Out of the

Ireland Then and Now

JOHN A. BRENNAN

Out of the Ice

Ireland Then and Now

JOHN A. BRENNAN

Escribe Publishing Inc.

New York

Dedication

This book is dedicated to all who went before and paved the road.

Praise for Out of the Ice

"John A. Brennan's attention to historic detail and his references to the ancient writings supporting this history lend to a seasoned, logical progression of events that does more than document dates and peoples, but charts what each group brought to the country to help build the Irish culture we know today. This approach offers far more insights than the traditional historical focus on events, delving into the influences and ideas behind the modern Irish psyche."

Diane Donovan
Midwest Review
September 2017 Review Issue

Table of Contents

Acknowledgements

During the research phase of this book about early Ireland, I've relied on the writings of Michael O'Cleary, a Franciscan monk, who, with three other scholars, compiled what has collectively become known as the "Annals of The Four Masters." The annals, written in a Franciscan Friary in Donegal town between 1632 AD and 1636 AD, are a compilation of the ancient writings that were saved from destruction and tell the story of Ireland from the end of the last ice age, up to the mid-1600s.

I have also accessed Geoffrey Keating's invaluable 'History of Ireland.' I gathered further information from the "Annals of Ulster," the "Book of Armagh," the "Annals of Clonmacnoise," the "Book of Invasions" and the "Book of Leinster."

John A. Brennan

Preface

The research phase for this book swept me up and took me on a fascinating, personal and deeply spiritual journey, back through the shrouded mists of time and space, revealing an Ireland that I did not know existed. Accessing, studying and understanding the many ancient writings was a long and intensive undertaking, but the more I read, the more I realized that I was fully enjoying the experience and I allowed myself to become totally immersed.

My main purpose in writing this book was to educate myself first and secondly, to pass on what I have learned to anyone wishing to know about the land of their forefathers, without having to laboriously peruse and decipher the myriad of old, dusty annals, which I have done on their behalf. See this book as a History of Ireland for those too busy with their day to day lives, to devote the time and effort needed to research the ancient story. My hope is that anyone who reads this book will learn as much about Ireland as I did and be equally fascinated.

Introduction

This book is **not** the work of an academic, rather it is the humble attempt by a man who believes that he is deeply connected to and influenced by the spirit and essence of his ancestors. Unlike the wide array of other books recounting the history of Ireland and written with much detail and scholarly facts, this book seeks to inform the reader of some of the **lesser** known, but extremely important events which are vital to the story of how Ireland became the country that it is today.

According to the writings in many of the ancient Annals, much of the world, including Ireland, was covered with vast ice sheets until approximately 11,000 years ago. As the ice slowly retreated it carved the island into the shape that it is today. Once the weight and pressure of the ice was no longer a factor the earth sprang back and major volcanic activity took place. When these eruptions finally ceased the earth cooled, water rose to the surface and became the lakes and rivers that today we all know and love. Over time, the island became covered in dense oak, birch and ash forests and herds of deer, packs of wolves and wild boar roamed freely, waiting patiently for her first human visitors…

Chapter 1
The Beginning

The Beginning

According to the writings in many of the ancient annals, much of the world including Ireland was covered with vast ice sheets until approximately 11,000 years ago. As global temperatures rose, the ice slowly retreated and carved the island into the shape that it is today. Once the weight and pressure of the ice was no longer a factor the earth sprang back and major volcanic activity took place. When these eruptions finally ceased the earth cooled, water rose to the surface and became the lakes and rivers that today we all know and love.

It is thought that the first humans arrived in Ireland around 9000 years ago and are believed to have crossed land bridges that still existed at that time. One bridge connected southeastern Ireland and southwestern Britain; the other connected County Antrim in northeastern Ireland with the west coast of Scotland. Across these land bridges came bands of various hunter gatherers whose numbers were so small that they made little impact and soon died out from disease and starvation. Several species of wild animals migrated around this time also, the most notable being the giant elk. The elk was almost big as an elephant and a perfect specimen can be seen in the National Museum in Dublin.

Recently, fossil remains of extremely large bears have been found in caves in Ireland and suggests by means of DNA sampling, that they are possibly the forebears of our modern Polar bear. Wild boar and herds of deer roamed the forests where packs of wolves lived and hunted freely. There is archaeological evidence that County Antrim was the favored area of habitation as this northern part of Ireland was the only source of flint, which the stone-age people utilized as tools, arrow heads and spear points. These hunter gatherers lived mostly along the coasts, ate fish and fowl and rarely ventured inland. Ireland was covered in dense oak, birch and ash forests at that time and as the sea level rose, the land bridges disappeared, trapping the larger animals, which eventually led to their extinction. This period became known as the Mesolithic stone-age.

1   Cessair

According to many of the old writings, the first individually named human to make an impact in Ireland was Cessair, a daughter of the biblical Noah's son Bith and his wife Birren, who were denied a place on the Ark. Cessair, together with three men and fifty women, set sail on their own. In some versions of the tale, Noah tells them to go to the western edge of the world to escape the oncoming Flood. In other versions, when their people are denied a place on Noah's Ark, Cessair tells them to make an idol to advise them. This idol tells them to escape the Flood by sailing to Ireland. They set out in three ships and reach Ireland after a long, seven year journey. However, when they attempt to land, two of the ships are lost. The only survivors are Cessair, forty-nine other women, and three men: Fintan mac Bóchra, Bith and Ladra. They land in Ireland at Bantry Bay forty days before the Flood, in the age of the World 2242, according to the Annals of the Four Masters, but their numbers were too small to completely inhabit the land. Cessair is said to be buried at the summit of Knockmaa, near Tuam, County Galway.

2   Fomorians

Next to arrive were the Fomorians who were reportedly seafarers, possibly pirates. It is written that they originally came from Northern Africa or Carthage and are described as having dark hair and skin. They are said to be the first people to inhabit Ireland during the time of the great flood. They, together with their leader Cichol Gricenchos, arrived two hundred years before the next race, the Partholonians. By all accounts they were a warlike and troublesome people and ruled their followers with iron fists. The Fomorians seem to have been a race that brought the harmful and destructive powers of nature, chaos, darkness, death, blight and drought.

3   Partholon

A group led by Partholon, a son of Sera, the King of Greece came next, making this the first mention of royalty in Irish history. This group was the first to arrive after the time of the great flood. They arrive on the uninhabited island and are responsible for introducing such things as farming, cooking, brewing and stone-buildings. It was during this time Newgrange passage tomb was built along with many other stone mounds, cairns and passage graves. The Book of Invasions gives us a little more information stating that Partholon and one thousand followers came to Ireland via Greece, Sicily and Anatolia arriving roughly about 300 years after the great flood. At the time of their arrival there were three lakes, nine rivers and one large plain. Their numbers grew to approximately four thousand but were eventually to become victims of a plague. It is believed that Parthalon fought the Fomorians in the first battle on Irish soil. Parthalon cleared four more plains and seven more lakes formed.

The Lebor Gabála Érenn, an 11th-century Christian pseudo-history of Ireland, says that Ireland was settled six times, with Partholón and his followers being the second group. According to the Lebor Gabála, Ireland was uninhabited following the deaths of Cessair and her companions. It tells us that Partholón came from Greece and was the son of Sera, son of Sru, a descendant of Magog, son of Japheth, son of Noah. Partholón and his people sail to Ireland via Sicily and Iberia, arriving 300 or 312 years after the flood and landing at Inber Scéne (Kenmare in County Kerry). With

Partholón were his wife Delgnat, their three sons, Slanga, Rudraige and Laiglinne, their wives Nerba, Cichba and Cerbnad, and a thousand followers.

4   Nemedians

When the Nemedians arrived Ireland had been largely uninhabited for many years following the deaths of Partholon's last followers. Some small pockets of Fomorians still survived but were defeated by the Nemedians in three epic battles and driven back and moved out onto Tory Island off the north-west coast. After they had travelled for a year and a half, the Nemedians arrived in Ireland with only one intact ship. Also on board are his wife Macha, his four chieftain sons (Starn, Iarbonel, Annind, and Fergus.) Nemed's wife Macha, died twelve days after they arrived and is buried at Ard Mhacha (Armagh.) According to the Lebor Gabála, Nemed, like those who settled Ireland before him, had a genealogy going back to the biblical Noah. He and three thousand of his people later died from the effects of a plague. All but thirty of Nemed's people were wiped out. Of this thirty, one group flees "into the north of the world", one group flees to Britain, and another group flees to Greece. Those who went into the north become the Tuatha Dé Danann (or Tuath Dé), the main pagan gods of Ireland. Nemed was buried on the hill of Ard Nemid on Great Island in Cork Harbor.

5   Fir Bolg

The Fir Bolg are descendants of the people of Nemed, who inhabited Ireland before them. After leaving Ireland, some of Nemed's remaining followers arrived in Greece. The annals say that they were enslaved by the Greeks and made to carry bags of soil or clay, hence the name 'Fir Bolg' (men of bags). They were forced to settle on poor, rocky land but that they made it into fertile fields by dumping great amounts of soil on it. After 230 years of slavery, they leave Greece at the same time as the Israelites left Egypt. In a great fleet, the Fir Bolg sail to Iberia and then on to Ireland. Led by their five chieftains, they divide Ireland into five provinces: Gann takes

North Munster, Sengann takes South Munster, Genann takes Connacht, Rudraige takes Ulster and Slánga takes Leinster. They establish the High Kingship and a succession of nine High Kings rule over Ireland for the next 37 years. The last High King, Eochaid mac Eirc, is the example of a perfect king. The Fir Bolg are also said to contain two sub-groups known as the Fir Domnann and Fir Gáilióin.

The Fir Bolg were ejected from Ireland at one point, but returned some time later from Scotland, with a leader called Aengus and this episode is loosely referred to as a 'Pictish' invasion. They were given the Aran Islands on which they settled and there are remnants of a fortress on Inishmore related to Aengus and the Fir Bolg. With the Fir Bolg came the first quasi Celtic influence.

6   Tuatha De Dannan

Our history becomes more interesting when the Tuatha De Danann arrive. The Tuatha De Dannan, translated as 'peoples of the Goddess Danu,' were a supernatural race who came to Ireland with the intention of removing the evil Fomorians, a race that already inhabited the island and who caused widespread destruction and mayhem. The Tuatha were divided into three tribes, the tribe of 'Tuatha,' the nobility, the tribe of 'De,' the priests and the tribe of 'Danann,' the bards, storytellers and minstrels.

The art of storytelling in Ireland began with the Tuatha and has been handed down through each successive generation until the present day. This new race were the descendants of Nemed and it is believed that among their possessions were four magical treasures: The Dagda's cauldron, The Spear of Lugh, The Stone of Fal and The Sword of light of Nuada. Epic battles were fought against the remnants of the Fir Bolg and the remaining Fomorians. Led by their King Nuada, they fought the Fir Bolg in two great battles and defeated them. Many of the myths and legends that we are all familiar with, started to take root at this time. Lugh, the Tuatha champion was then crowned king.

7   Milesians

Next, came the Milesians led by Ith who was the son of a Scythian father named Goidel Glas and who, it is said, was present at the fall of the Tower of Babel, and whose mother Scota, was a Pharoah's daughter. She was rumored to be a daughter of either Thutmose III or Amenhotep II who were simultaneous Pharaoh's at the time of the exodus of the Israelites. The Milesians left Egypt around the time of the exodus and eventually settled in the Iberian Peninsula (Galicia and Northern Portugal). Legend has it that Ith first saw Ireland from the top of Hercules tower in Galicia. Many epic battles were fought between the Milesians and the Tuatha De Dannan. Eventually, a deal was struck whereby the land was divided, with the clever Milesians getting the above ground and the Tuatha the underground. It is from this time we start to hear the stories about the little people and the fairies.

8   Arrival of Agriculture

The practice of farming had spread from the Middle East through eastern and southern Europe and reached the British Isles around 6000 years ago. It arrived in Ireland with the settlers who came next, 5500 years ago. These Neolithic people brought goats, sheep and cattle, wheat and barley. One very important discovery was Porcellanite, a stone harder and more durable than flint, which the Mesolithic people had used. With axes made from this harder stone the upland forests were able to be cleared effectively. Thus, during the Neolithic stone-age, basic farming began in Ireland. The discovery of metal was another major turning point in human history and this new technology arrived in Ireland approximately 4000 years ago. It is believed that settlers from France (Gaels?) brought it with them and slowly the existing inhabitants learned how to mix copper and tin. These two cultures merged and gave birth to the Irish Bronze age. It would be wrong to assume that the Mesolithic people of Ireland suddenly invented farming and became Neolithic. Instead, Ireland's Mesolithic hunter/gatherers were displaced or assimilated by the new Neolithic settlers who gradually arrived in Ireland from Britain and brought the technology with them. It seems that it arrived in Ireland via the Scotland-Antrim link between 3900BC and 3000BC.

9   The Celts

Celts began arriving in Ireland around 2500 years ago and it was during this period that my ancestors, the O'Brannains arrived. One of the major advantages the Celts possessed was their discovery of Iron. They came in such large numbers that within a few hundred years of their arrival, they either obliterated or assimilated the existing cultures. It is thought that as the Romans advanced slowly westward, the Celts moved ahead of the legions and some of these tribes ended up in Ireland. They could not retreat further. Hibernia, as Ireland became known, was their last bastion. Others went north and settled in Scotland, more migrated south to Cornwall and Devon, some settled in Wales.

With these Celts came a tribe called the Romanies, who it is said had the gift of second sight. A priestly sect known as Druids also migrated with the main body of Celts and would eventually have a huge impact on the direction that Irish culture took from this time. Ireland and the area of Scotland north of Hadrian's Wall were never conquered by the Romans, they did, however, set up trading posts in Ireland but not until approximately 100 AD. It appears that the Romans influenced the language of at least one Celtic clan in Munster as they spoke Latin. The ancient Ogham was the first written script in Ireland, was based on the Latin alphabet and resembled a runic style of writing, but distinctly Celtic.

After the fall of the Roman Empire the greater part of Europe descended into utter chaos and this period became known as the dark ages. Anarchy ruled, all learning waned and book burning was common. Ireland however, being an insular island, ignored all of this and continued to flourish academically and intellectually. Scholar monks, fluent in Gaelic, Latin, Greek and Hebrew with their foresight and unremitting dedication, kept scholarship alive. Ireland in the 5th century was the center of scholastic learning and the term 'Land of Saints and Scholars' describes this perfectly, for that's what Ireland was then and still is today.

Chapter 2
Poets and Poetry in Ireland

1   The Oral Tradition

"And there are among them composers of verses whom they call Bards; these singing to instruments similar to a lyre, applaud some, while they vituperate others."
Diodorus Siculus, 8 BCE

All poets have the uncanny ability to tap into the realm of spirit, the realm where all inspiration emanates. It is a gift that enables us to transcend the mundane, and experience the world as we see and feel it, and know how it should be. We are magicians and have the uncanny ability to turn what to most people, are chaotic thoughts, emotions and feelings, and fashion them into beautiful and meaningful works of art. We paint the blank canvas with our words and are blessed with the grace that enables us to never stray far from our original nature, despite having to live and survive in the material world. We poets pass on what we have learned through our words, which are the manifestation of our collective knowledge. It is a shamanistic quality which we possess. All cultures revere their poets, none more so than my own, the Irish, we call them Seanacchie (shan-a-key) meaning the storytellers, the bards and the minstrels.

It is widely accepted that both the oral tradition of storytelling, and the early written works of ancient Ireland are among the most original and earliest forms of communication in Europe. Poetry in Ireland has survived the ravages of time for two main reasons. Firstly, Ireland sits in the Atlantic Ocean, on the westernmost edge of Europe and thus insulated from much of the happenings elsewhere on the continent. From the end of the last ice-age until the 4th century it enjoyed relative peace and solitude and remained unscathed even when the violent legions of the Roman empire swept across the world conquering towns and villages and imposing Roman law.

Secondly, prior to the 4th century, writing had not yet been developed in Ireland and all important information such as history and lore was memorized and passed down orally through the generations by master storytellers from father to son. Even after literacy took hold in the 4th century, and much was written down by scribes and monks in the monasteries, the old tradition was kept alive and is still used today. The thinking at that time may have been that if you put your words on paper you run the risk of them being lost or destroyed. This did actually happen when the Saxons raided Ireland in 686 AD and again when Viking marauders struck in 798 AD.

The first mention of the storytelling tradition in Ireland, is found in the one of the old annals called the 'Book of Invasions.' The tradition begins with the Tuatha De Dannan, a race of people who inhabited Ireland well before the beginning of western civilization, and has been handed down ever since through each successive generation. The name Tuatha De Dannan means "people of the goddess Danu." They were a supernatural race who came to Ireland with the intention of removing the evil Fomorians, a race that already inhabited the island and who caused destruction and mayhem. The Tuatha were divided into three tribes, the tribe of Tuatha who were the nobility, the tribe of De, the priests and the tribe of Danann, the bards and storytellers. In medieval Ireland, there was a distinct hierarchy in the poetic tradition. Two groups of Poets existed, the Ollamh and the Bard, and each group took their respective places side by side, in the recounting of all important Irish affairs. A poet in Irish society was revered, held a privileged position and was granted special rights regarding property and immunity from many legal issues.

2   The Filid

The name Filid (seer) comes from the same root as the Welsh word meaning "to see," and is a collective term given to all Irish poets and storytellers. It is believed, that originally they were all powerful, holding high office as magicians, lawgivers, judges, advisors to the kings, composers and poets. Later, after a fundamental change occurred, the Brehons took over the position of lawmakers, and all other legal matters. Another group, the Druids took over as priests and handled all supernatural matters. Filid then became the master poets and philosophers, being mostly concerned with language, and court poetry. They held a very prestigious social position in Celtic Ireland and worked side by side with and in support of the Druids as they carried out their duties. There were seven grades of Filid, the most important being the Ollam (pronounced olav) and the lowest position taken by the Bard.

The Filid were made up of a large, aristocratic class and as professional poets, could and did command payment. Some charged large fees for their services and made good use of what was known as the 'Poet's curse' to ensure their continued power and of course, employment. It was firmly believed that a well composed verse could ruin a person's reputation and cause harm and even hasten the death of an individual. Of course as with all matters pertaining to the human condition, some Filid overstepped the boundaries and were taken to task for their infractions. In the latter half of the 6th century the 'Synod of Drumceta' was convened. During the Synod, many of the Filid were indeed accused of abusing their power and influence with the nobility in efforts to further their own aims.

Fortunately, one of their major defenders at the Synod was Colmcille (St. Columba) the 6th century Irish scholar monk. Colmcille was the dominant figure in early Christian Ireland, active in all affairs, was a revered scholar and a force to be reckoned with. Even though a Filid could be penalized for abusing his position, belief in the "Poet's Curse" was so widespread and powerful, few were rarely punished, and their legacy has survived right up to modern times. Another asset in their arsenal was the fact that they were closely aligned with monasteries, which were the seats of learning, and with Colmcille's blessing, they survived the inquisition and prospered. Filid held a very responsible position in Ireland and among their many official duties they were obligated to teach the residents of their respective area in all aspects of literature, folklore and the history of the country. These small schools would later become the Bardic colleges. By the 12th century Filid were writing nature poetry and poems of a personal nature, in praise of their benefactors more human attributes rather than their skills in battle and heroic deeds.

3   The Ollamh

An Ollamh (pronounced ulav) had to devote as many as twelve years of his life to studying and learning and by the end of his apprenticeship he would have memorized more than three hundred different meters, at least two hundred main stories and about one hundred lesser stories. The apprenticeship employed the use of sensory deprivation and the novice would spend long periods of time alone in a dark cell with nothing but his own mind for company. It was believed that in this way only, could the higher realm be accessed, the place where all inspiration emanates. When his learning period was complete, he was then allowed to wear the coveted 'cloak of crimson bird feathers' and carry a wand of office. The most widely used form of poem used by the Ollamh was known as the *Deibide*, which means "cut in half," and was a quatrain made up of two couplets joined by rhyming one stressed syllable and one syllable not stressed.

The term Ollamh was a title given to the highest ranking member of the Filid, and set him apart from the others, signifying a "person of great learning." It is a term also used to refer to the highest member of any group, so for example, an Ollamh *brithem* would be the highest rank of judge and an Ollamh *Rí* would be the highest rank of king. Typically, a 'Chief Ollamh of Poetry' was considered equal to the king and could therefore wear the six colors worn by the nobility. He sat at the King's table and even ate from the same dishes as the king denoting his stature and importance. One of the most famous Ollamhs was a poet named Ollav Fala, the eighteenth descendant of Érimón who lived around 1000 BC.

An Ollamh Ri ('most high') was the chief poet of literature and history. Each province had its own Ollamh Ri and would be employed by the local chieftain or noble. The Ollamh Ri would be in charge of all other Ollamhs in his province. He had his own 'great house' and could have as many as thirty Ollamhs under his charge. In our modern society, the title, Ollamh Ri is equivalent to a combination of today's Minister of Education and Culture and Poet Laureate. His father, and probably his grandfather too, would have held the same position, making it a hereditary post, handed down. Prior to the 6th century, the Ollamh Ri was appointed by the king but after that date elections were held in which the other Ollamhs of the province voted him into office.

4   The Bard

The Bard was a professional poet and musician, trained in the 'Bardic Schools of Ireland' and was employed by a king, chieftain or nobleman. His role was to compose poems and songs to glorify the virtues of his employer and family. As officials of the court of king or chieftain, they performed a number of official roles. Bards were considered lesser than the Ollamh but were renowned performers and entertainers, and were also revered as teachers. Both Bards and Ollamhs used meter and rhyme as a way of memorizing their words. The Bard memorized and preserved the history and traditions of their clan and country, as well as the technical requirements of the various poetic forms, such as syllabic, assonance, half rhyme and alliteration. Both Ollamh and Bard would also be required to study, understand and be fully versed with the Ogham tree-alphabet when it arrived later on In Ireland.

The Bard would be familiar with the history of the royal family, his own clan members and the country and would compose eulogies. They were chroniclers and satirists whose job it was to praise their employers and curse anyone who dared to anger them. It was believed that a well-aimed poem, could cause blisters to break out on the face of its target, so sharp and direct were the words. It has been recorded that Bards had the power to settle arguments and even intervene in violent confrontations, and using their words, defuse the situation. It has been speculated that the differences between Ollamhs and Bards may have originated when Christianity gained a foothold in the 5th century. One theory, widely believed, is that the Ollamhs were more in line with the new church and composed many prayers and hymns. Although Bards were seen as somewhat lesser than the Ollamhs, their influence has endured as modern Ireland continues the age-old tradition of storytelling.

5   The Limerick

Croom, County Limerick is a small 4th century village located on the banks of the River Maigue. Although now having a tidal flow only to the town of Adare, in ancient times the river had a tidal flow past Croom, making it a convenient route for the Viking ships sailing inland from the River Shannon, during the 9th and 10th centuries. Contacts made along the Maigue River between those marauders and the clan O'Donovan provides us with details of the alliance between the two groups, in the late 10th century.

An important school of poetry was born in Croom in the early 18th century, and the poets who met there wrote and recited their works in Gaelic. A new form of verse was also founded in Croom by two notable bards who grew up together and were lifelong friends. This new form became known as the Limerick, named after the County of Limerick.

The two founders of the Limerick, were Maigue Poets Sean O' Tuama and his friend Andrias MacRaith. Both men grew up and were educated together near the small town of Kilmallock, Co. Limerick. A large part of their education came from local Hedgemasters.

Aindrias MacCraith 1710-1795

Born near Croom, County Limerick, MacCraith was a poet and wandering minstrel known as 'The Wandering Peddler'. He was one of the leading poets of the Maigue school. Like many of these Gaelic poets, they supported the Jacobean cause and, like so many others, got into trouble with the authorities and were forced to leave the neighborhood. One of MacCraith's most famous works was the eulogy he composed in honor of his fellow poet Seán Ó Tuama. Aindrias MacCraith is buried in County Limerick.

Seán Ó Tuama c. 1706-1775

Born near Kilmallock, County Limerick, O'Tuama was a school teacher and a leading member of the Poets of the Maigue. He also ran an inn that became a well-known meeting place for the local poets. The inn is opposite the church where he is buried. His best known poem is 'A Chuisle na hÉigse'. After the two men had a falling out (probably over a woman), they began castigating each other in rhyme.

Below are believed to be the first Limericks ever written and predate Edward Lear by almost one hundred years. O' Tuama is buried in Croom, Co. Limerick.

O'Tuama wrote:
"I sell the best Brandy and Sherry
to make all my customers merry.
But at times their finances
run short as it chances.
And then I feel sad, very very."

MacCraith replied:
"O'Tuama, you boast yourself handy,
at selling good ale and bright Brandy,
But the fact is your liquor
makes everyone sicker
I tell you this I, your good friend Andy."

6   Ogham

Ogham is a medieval alphabet which was used to write on trees and stone and was an early Irish language widely used until about the 9th century. One possible origin of the word ogham is from the Irish *og-úaim* 'point-seam', referring to the seam made by the point of a sharp weapon as it carved on wood and stone. According to many of the ancient manuscripts, Ogham was first invented along with the Gaelic language soon after the fall of the Tower of Babel, by the legendary Scythian King Fenius Farsa. The story goes that Fenius journeyed from Scythia together with Goídel mac Ethéoir, and a following of seventy-two scholars. They came to the dusty plain of Shinar to study the babbling languages spoken at Nimrod's tower, which was also known as the Tower of Babel. Finding that the languages had already been distributed, Fenius sent his scholars far and wide to study them and stayed behind at the tower awaiting their eventual return. After ten years had elapsed, the investigations were complete, and Fenius created "the chosen language", by taking the best of each of the confusing tongues, putting them together and creating a new form which he called 'Goídelc.' He also created Ogham as a perfected writing system for his languages. The names he gave to the letters of his alphabet were those of his 25 best scholars.

Another story tells of the 'Ogham Tract' and credits an individual named Ogma with the script's invention. Ogma was skilled in speech and poetry, and is said to have created the system for those who had some literacy. The first message reputedly written in Ogham were seven letter 'b's' carved on a birch tree. It was a warning to a local chieftain, deciphered as meaning: "your wife will be carried away seven times to the otherworld unless the birch protects her." For this reason, the letter 'b' is said to be named after the birch tree. Even after it ceased to be used as an everyday alphabet for writing, Ogham continued to be used as the basis for teaching grammar and the rules and metrics of poetry in the Gaelic language. The medieval book, 'The Scholar's Primer' set out the basics for writing poetry in the Irish language for the trainee Ollamh or Bard, and used Ogham as a guide as the ogham alphabet was felt to be peculiarly suited to the needs of the Irish language.

7   The Decline

Christianity came to Ireland in the late 4th century and almost immediately set out to convert the whole island. One side effect of this conversion was the strain it put on the coffers of the Chiefs and Noblemen. As more and more monasteries and later churches, sprung up and the new religion took a firm hold, the nobility were expected to provide land and titles for the church leaders. By the 6th century, already stretched to the limit with the ever-increasing costs of frequent inter-tribal conflicts, a far reaching decision was made to cut the number of Filid employed by many of the clans, in an effort to curb expenditure. Not a popular decision among the wordsmiths I am sure, but sadly, at the time it was deemed a necessity. From the 12th century onwards Celtic culture suffered a rapid decline as a direct result of the invasion by the Normans. The new invaders were fully literate and preferred the written word as opposed to the oral tradition. This so called high society lasted right up to the time of the reign of Elizabeth 1. Eventually, the new form of literature replaced the old familiar style used for centuries by the ancient Ollamhs and Bards. In spite of all of this upheaval, the old system lasted until the middle of the 17th century, but declined rapidly during the time of the Tudor re-conquest.

After their defeat at the Battle of Kinsale in 1601, and the end of the Nine Years' War in Ulster in 1603, Hugh O'Neill, the Earl of Tyrone and Rory O'Donnell, the Earl of Tyrconnell together with many other noblemen were forced into exile by the English government who now ruled Ireland, under the leadership of Lord Mountjoy. The land had been laid to waste due to the violent destruction and a countrywide famine devastated the population. For many, the end of the world had finally arrived.
On September 14, 1607, the Earls and their many followers left Ireland for Spain. Their plan was to enlist a new army in France and Spain and return to Ireland to oust the English settlers who had taken their titles and lands. Unfortunately, O'Neil and O'Donnell both died in exile and the planned return to Ireland and subsequent rebellion, never took place. This singular event was the death knell for the age-old tradition of the Filid and their centuries old connection with the Irish nobility. The old tradition however, was not obliterated completely thanks to the birth of Hedge Schools in the 17th century. Today, modern Ireland continues the old tradition with the worldwide popularity of a plethora of celebrated Irish poets, musicians and playwrights.

8   The Last Ollam.

> *"In Creggan graveyard I slept last night in despair.*
> *With the rising of the morning a woman came to me with a kiss.*
> *Bright burning were her cheeks and her hair shone like gold.*
> *It would be medicine to the world to behold that young Queen. "*

Those words are from the poem "Creggan Graveyard" written by Ollam Art McCooey, the last of the five Gaelic poets of the province of south east Ulster. He was also known as "Art of the Songs" and was the chief Ollam attached to the royal household of the O'Neill clan, the rulers of a barony in south Armagh called "The Fews." Art McCooey was born sometime in the early 1700's, in a townland close to my hometown of Crossmaglen. The area known today as Mounthill, sits near to the old church at Creggan, and what remains of a castle at Glassdrummond, both built by Henry Og O'Neill, the Lord of the Fews. He died on January 7, 1773 and is buried in Creggan graveyard, close to the O'Neill family vault.

9   Hedge Schools

In 1603 James VI of Scotland ascended to both the English and Irish thrones. He became known as James I of Ireland and immediately a series of repressive new laws were enacted. These new laws became known as the Penal Laws. From 1607, Catholics were barred from holding public office or serving in the Irish Army. All Catholic churches were brought under the control of the Anglican church, which was considered to be the true church. Catholic priests were tolerated for a short period, but bishops were forced to operate in secret. Later, more repressive laws outlawed the Priests as well and the dreaded Priest Hunters scoured the land in search of the hidden Priests, who now had a bounty on their heads.
Schools were not permitted to teach the Irish language or history and were strictly controlled. The new monarch's aim was to eradicate Catholicism in one generation. Out of all of this mayhem the Hedge Schools were born, purely in retaliation to the harsh Penal Laws. The first of those laws stipulated that "no person of the popish religion shall publicly or in private houses teach school, or instruct youth in learning within this realm..."

The English government did set up Charter schools but the Catholic population refused to use them as they were seen as an attempt to Anglicize the children. Those who could afford the Hedgemaster's fees sent their children to Hedge Schools where Brehons, Bards, storytellers and musicians secretly taught Irish history, tradition, poetry, and told tales of their ancestors. Mathematics, geography, world history along with all other subjects taught in the state sponsored schools, were taught in the Hedge Schools too. In the beginning, both adults and children would meet secretly in old dilapidated buildings, behind old walls or in ditches along the roadside. Some lessons were actually taught in the hedgerows, giving rise to the name Hedge School. Other schools met in old barns and outhouses. In this way, despite the efforts of the English government to wipe the slate clean of all things Irish, we as a people survived. In the final analysis, we owe a huge debt of gratitude to those brave Hedgemasters, who, at great risk to their own lives, kept the culture alive.

Chapter 3
Regicide and New Beginnings

1   The Slaughter at Magh Cru. (Field of Blood.)

The following story tells of a significant event which took place in Ireland during the latter half of the 1st century AD, and which set in motion a chain of events that would influence and forever change the political and economic landscapes of Ireland, Britain and Scotland. The event involved three Kings, who together with their many nobles and attendants, had assembled at a fortress in the western province of Connaught, Ireland. The reason for the gathering, a sumptuous banquet, was conceived by a rural Chieftain, meticulously planned in minute detail, and took three years of careful preparation. As soon as details had been finalized, invitations were dispatched and delivered by couriers.

The reigning high King of Ireland Fiachaidh Fionnoladh, a descendant from a long line of the Milesian nobility, his wife Eithne, daughter of the King of Scotland; Feig, son of Fidheic Caoch, King of Munster, whose wife was Beartha, daughter of Goirtniad, King of Britain; Breasal, son of Firb, King of Ulster, whose wife Aine, was the daughter of the King of Sacsa, her father's name was Cainneall, accepted the invitations and traveled with their respective retinues, in two-wheeled chariots, horse drawn carts, horseback and on foot, meeting en-masse, on an open plain below the imposing stronghold of 'Magh Cru.' As their attendants led the horses to the stables, the retinue proceeded up the ramp, crossed the earthen ditches, were met by the ever alert gatekeepers, and escorted to the entrance of the great hall.

The great hall, with its thick walls and oak roof beams, was laid out in readiness for the hungry guests, where rows of flickering birch-twig torches, wrapped in sheep's wool dipped in beeswax, gave off a warm, inviting glow. The walls, usually displaying an array of battleaxes and broadswords, were instead adorned with colorful banners and woolen fabrics, reaching all the way to the vaulted ceiling, high above the wooden, plank floor. Sturdy trestles supported the tables lining the walls on either side, resplendent with large platters, piled high with roasted wild boar, beef, venison, mutton, salmon and jugs of ale and mead. The wall at the far end of the long hall was dominated by a large, open fireplace that crackled noisily and sent plumes of smoke and fiery sparks up through the wide chimney. Stacked close to the hearth were piles of dried peat blocks and seasoned logs, enough fuel to keep the fire burning well into the night.

To the left of the fireplace sat a small table, reserved for the *Ollamhs*, scribes associated with the High King and his clan, their birch-bark parchments and styli, already laid out neatly in readiness for recording the evenings events. Careful note of the names of all in attendance would be taken, using the newly developed *ogham* inscription system. Behind the small table and near to the corner, concealed behind a long wall hanging, was the flight-door, a small exit which could be used for escape in times of trouble. The doorway opened onto a stone stairway which led to a dark, narrow, passageway (*souterrain*) that ran underground and came up under a trapdoor, set in one corner of the stable floor. To the right of the fireplace were benches where the bards and minstrels would sit, waiting their turn to entertain the audience with word and song, their harps and *bodhrans* tuned and ready.

As was the custom, females were assigned a separate hall in which they were served and attended to and which would turn out to have far reaching effects on future events in the aftermath of the nights gathering. Another custom stipulated that before the guests were admitted, the banquet-hall was cleared, so that only three people remained within. The three who remained were the *Seanchas*, similar to our present day master of ceremonies; the *Bollsaire*, the marshal of the premises and a Trumpeter who would summon the guests. All three stood inside to the right of the entrance doors, then, when everything was ready, the trumpet would sound to call the shield bearers of the kings, their nobles and attendants. Each

Issued

ITEM(S)	DUE DATE
Dragon rider DCPL9000076100	24 Jan 2023
Selkie warrior DCPL9000076110	24 Jan 2023
The story of the Irish r... DCPL0000306142	24 Jan 2023
Out of the ice : Ireland... DCPL9000042170 Renewals (2)	24 Jan 2023

Your current loan(s): 4
Your current reservation(s): 0
Your current active request(s): 0

To renew your items please log onto
My Account at
https://dublincity.spydus.ie

Thank you for using your local
library.

bearer in turn, would hand the shield, emblazoned with a coat of arms, to the *Bollsaire* who, directed by the *Seanchas*, would then hang it on one of the iron hooks that protruded, at intervals, from the walls above the seats. When the trumpet sounded a second time, the shields of the rural Chieftains and their followers, were hung on the opposite wall above their seats. When the trumpet sounded a third time, everyone entered the banquet-hall and took their seats beneath his own shield. The gatekeepers then swung the heavy, wooden doors shut, the large iron hinges creaking as they slowly closed. Large barrel bolts were slid into place and a stout wooden brace was dropped in position. The great hall was secure and the stage was set for what was to follow.

The hosts of the banquet on that fateful night were three renegade chieftains of the *Attacotti* tribe, named Monach, Buan, and Cairbre Caitcheann. Of the three, Cairbre, known as 'cat head,' was the more vengeful and ruthless individual. He was a descendant of the Fir Bolg, a lowly, violent race that had inhabited Ireland much earlier. Before arriving in Ireland, the Fir Bolg (men of bags) had been made slaves by their masters, the Greeks, and forced to carry and distribute bags of soil in barren areas in an effort to create new tracts of arable land. In serfdom for more than two hundred years, they planned and staged a violent revolt against their oppressors and after slaughtering and robbing them, commandeered several ships and set sail, eventually arriving in Ireland. In time they established a Kingship and a succession of nine Fir Bolg kings ruled over Ireland for many generations. Following a prolonged series of pitched battles, the Fir Bolg were finally ejected from Ireland, but returned some time later from Scotland, with a leader called Aengus, an episode loosely referred to as a 'Pictish' invasion. They were forced onto the Aran Islands on which they settled, and where remnants of a fortress on Inishmore, related to Aengus and the Fir Bolg, can still be seen.

Regular incursions were made onto the mainland in attempts to recover their former positions of power, but as they were too few in number, it was impossible for them to re-gain control. In the end, they had to be satisfied with blending in with the ordinary people and grudgingly owe their allegiance to the elected king. Cairbre however, seething with vengeance, never gave up on his desire to re-establish power and avenge the perceived wrongs. Believing that he was the true heir to the kingship, he felt that his birthright had been taken illegally from his forebears, and was determined to retrieve the royal throne. Knowing that a full frontal assault would not be successful, he devised a cunning plan and for three years, cultivated relationships and formed alliances with two rogue chieftains who were well known to harbor ill feeling toward the ruling king and his followers. With promises of shares of the spoils and positions of power, the chieftains readily agreed to Cairbres' devious plot, and on the night of the banquet, Cairbre set his plan in motion.

In the great hall the feast was well underway, everybody had eaten their fill and the ale and mead flowed freely. Attendants, instructed to keep the drinking mugs filled, moved from table to table ensuring a steady flow. The revelers, relaxed and in high spirits, conversed with their fellow guests, and raucous laughter resounded and filled the great hall. Bards and minstrels, in their colorful cloaks, strolled among the tables singing the praises of the King and his clan members, the melodic sounds of their harps ringing and echoing off the walls. From the opposite side of the hall, Cairbre eyed his unsuspecting guests with careful deliberation; the time had arrived and now he would take his rightful place and restore honor, in the name of his ancestors. As pre-arranged, he rose slowly to his feet, removed his cloak and threw it onto the floor. His men, in unison, grabbed their swords and battle-axes, hidden earlier under their seats, and with blood curdling screams, leapt over the tables and charged the kings and their nobles. Surrounded, and with nowhere to run, Cairbre and his men proceeded to systematically slash and hack the unfortunate victims. Taken by surprise, and with no chance of escape, the kings, nobles and their attendants were overpowered and cut down in an unbridled orgy of violent savagery.

In the corner behind the scribes' table, the *Ollams* huddled together against the wall and watched helpless, as Cairbre grabbed the dead King Fiachaidh Fionnoladh by the hair, dragged his bloody body to the middle of the hall floor and with several blows of his axe, decapitate him. Monach and Buan grasped the lifeless bodies of Feig and Breasal and in an equally frenzied act of senseless butchery, severed their heads. Holding the heads aloft, they were met with a deafening roar of approval that reverberated off the walls, proclaiming the approval of the victors. The mutilated bodies of the nobles and attendants lay bleeding where they fell, on the floor, strewn across the tables, many still in their seats. Some ran towards the doors, hoping for escape, but were cut down with both axe and sword and lay dying, their blood seeping and staining the wooden planks. Shocked, but knowing he must keep his wits, the ard *Ollamh* quickly gathered the scrolls and hid them in an inner pocket of his cloak, then, his back to the wall, he inched slowly toward the corner, his mind racing. As he moved along, his foot caught on the fringe of the wall hanging covering the door to the tunnel. When he tried to free it, the fabric dislodged and fell to the floor, revealing the small door. Motioning to his fellow scribes he quickly opened the door and all three disappeared inside. Once inside, the door was shut and the three men hurried down the stone steps and ran blindly along the passage.

Off to one side of the great hall, on an elevated mound close to the stables, sat the small hall. Similar in construction to the great hall, it was generally used as a safe haven for women and children in times of unrest, but on that occasion it was used to accommodate the wives and servants of the visiting dignitaries. Although not designed to be as secure as the great hall, it was nevertheless strong enough to withstand any initial assault and the single, large door could be bolted from the inside, yet on this night it was deemed un-necessary. Inside, the women, terrified by the shouting and horrible screams coming from the great hall, clung together in fear. They were startled by the sudden sound of the door opening, and turning, were surprised but relieved to see the scribes and two stable attendants enter. Quickly, they guided the women out of the hall and helped them onto three waiting horse-drawn carts, and with no time to waste, moved rapidly toward the open entrance gates. The gatekeepers, already overpowered by the attendants, posed no threat, allowing the carts to disappear into the night. By the time Cairbre and his murderous henchmen reached the small hall, they found it silent and empty.

In the aftermath of the brutal extermination at 'Magh Cru,' Cairbre did indeed establish a kingship and ruled ineffectually until his sudden death, five years later. True to his word, he honored his promises to Monach and Buan and granted them lands and titles. The old annals tell us that Ireland suffered greatly following the events that took place on that unforgettable night. Civil unrest, severe drought and famines all made for terrible conditions throughout the island and the usurper Cairbre, despised and feared, was seen as the cause of all ills. On the death of his father, Cairbres' son Morann refused the throne and a lesser noble named Eilim became king and ruled for twenty years. The survivors who fled from Connaught on that night traveled to Scotland and found sanctuary with Eithne's father, the King of Scotland. Sometime later it was revealed that the murdered kings' wives were pregnant and eventually gave birth to three sons. Eithne named her son Tuathal Teachthmar; Beartha named her son Corb Olum and Aine, named her son Tibraide Tireach. Tuathal, being the son of Fiachaidh Fionnoladh, and following the true line of succession, was the rightful heir to the kingship of Ireland.

When news reached Ireland that the sons of the slain kings were alive, and after consultation with the Brehons and Druids, it was decided that envoys be sent to Scotland in an effort to encourage Tuathal to travel to Ireland and assume the sovereignty, which his father had held. Tuathal, by then aged twenty-five, agreed and with help from his grandfather and his followers, assembled a large army and set sail for Ireland at the end of the first century AD. He landed at Malahide, Dublin and proceeded to Tara, convened a Feis, and summoned the loyal clans and those others who supported his claim to the throne. His army, by then a considerable force, marched west and engaged Eilim and his forces in an all-out war for supremacy. At the Battle of Aichill, he defeated his enemy, slew most of their forces and set out on a countrywide campaign of subjugation. Tuathal Teachthmar, son of Fiachaidh Fionnoladh, was crowned high King of Ireland at Tara and reigned for thirty years, returning the line of Milesian nobility to its rightful place.

2 The Founding of Royal Midhe

If you ask, most people today will tell you, that there are four provinces in Ireland, namely, Ulster, Munster, Leinster and Connaught. What many people are not aware of is the fact that in the distant past, there were actually five provinces, the fifth one being the province called Royal Midhe.

At the beginning of the 2nd century A.D., and twenty-five years after the slaughter at 'Magh Cru' in Connaught, Tuathal Teachthmar, son of the slain high King, Fiachaidh Fionnoladh, traveled from Scotland to Ireland at the head of a large army and re-claimed the throne in the name of his father's Milesian forebears. After a series of country-wide, bloody battles against the rogue tribes, in which Tuathal was victorious, he was crowned Ard Ri of Ireland at the Stone of Fal, sited on a hill called Tara, in an area that we know today as county Meath. Tuathals' first official act as the new sovereign was to convene a *Feis* (general assembly) at which all nobles, chiefs and loyal clans would gather and swear allegiance to him and his descendants. At the *Feis*, sweeping new laws were established and the customs, annals and records were carefully noted and inscribed by the Ard *Ollamhs* in the Roll of Kings, also called the Psalter of Tara. Any previous law, custom or record not included in the Roll, was deemed to be false and irrelevant.

Tuathal, a visionary, knew that cohesion was key to his reign, now that he had united the disparate factions. He had to somehow hold the country together and ensure that a return to unrest and upheaval, caused by clan in-fighting, old grudges and disputes over land and property, would never be repeated. He knew instinctively that a form of centralized leadership would be the favorable way forward and after a series of meetings with his Nobles, Brehons, Druids and Ard Ollamhs, it was decided that a permanent seat of power be created. To fulfill this revolutionary idea, Tuathal annexed portions of territory from each of the four existing provinces and created a fifth. With Tara at its center, the new province was named *Midhe* and would be recognized as the seat of absolute Royal power, with Tuathal its undisputed sovereign.

Hill of Tiachtga

On the Hill of Ward, sited on land annexed from the province of Munster, and where the Druidess *Tiachtga*, daughter of the high Druid, *Mug Ruith*, was buried, Tuathal had a fortress constructed in her honor and re-named it the 'Hill of *Tiachtga*.' Built as an imposing ring-fort, it was surrounded by a deep earthen ditch, had a sturdy, exterior timber palisade that encircled the large enclosure, and heavy oak entrance gates. Inside, the great hall, stables, dwelling houses and storage areas were well protected and guarded at all times. There, every year, on the eve of *Samhain*, the Druids gathered and held their celebrations, the most important ceremony being the lighting of the first of the winter fires. The top of the hill was sacred ground and only accessible by the Druids, except on the Festival of *Samhain*, when members of the public were permitted. Local legend suggests that the Druids may have practiced human sacrifice at *Tiachtga* and it is thought that it later became a place of pilgrimage for women who were childless.

Samhain (sow-an) marks the end of the old year and the beginning of the new one. The Celtoi peoples further believed that this was a time of transition, when the veil between their world and the next was lifted, allowing the spirits of all who had died since the last *Oíche Shamhna* (Eve of *Samhain*) to make the transition to the next world. The Druids felt that this world and the otherworld were closest at Tlachtga and it was there that the festival of *Samhain*, (Halloween) was started. The old year's fires were extinguished and, after sunset, the ceremonial New Year *Samhain* fire was lit on the hill. Torches were lit from this sacred fire and carried to seven other hills around the county including Tara, Slane and Loughcrew, and then went on to light up the whole country.

Hill of Uisneach

On the Hill of *Uisneach*, in the portion taken from the province of Connaught, a second fortress was erected in a similar style as the one at *Tiachtga*. *Uisneach*, believed to be the geographical center of Ireland, was, until the reign of Tuathal, the place where all kings were crowned, and the ceremonial site of the celebrations of *Beltaine* (mayday.) *Beltaine* marked the beginning of summer, the time when the animals were driven out to the summer pastures. Rituals were performed to protect the cattle, crops and people, and to encourage growth. Special bonfires were kindled, and their flames, smoke and ashes were deemed to have protective powers. (It is believed that the Nemedian Druid, named Mide, lit the first fire there.) Countrywide, all household fires would be doused and then re-lit from the *Beltaine* bonfire. These gatherings would be accompanied by a feast, and some of the food and drink would be offered to the *aos sí* (fairies) to ensure a year of good luck and prosperity. In the province of Ulster, *Beltaine* was known as *Lammas*, and a fair has been held in Ballycastle, Co. Antrim, uninterrupted for more than three hundred years.

Today, *Uisneach* consists of a set of monuments and earthworks spread over two square kilometres. Around and upon the hill there are the remains of circular enclosures, barrows, cairns, a holy well and two ancient roads. On the southwest side of the hill is a large, oddly-shaped limestone rock inside a circular enclosure. It is almost 20 ft. tall and thought to weigh over 30 tons. In Gaelic it is called the *Ail na Míreann* (stone of the divisions,) and it is said to have been the place where the borders of all the provinces met.

Hill of Tailtiu

On land taken from the province of Ulster, Tuathal had a third fortress erected, again, similar in design to *Tiachtga* and *Uisneach*, it was dedicated to *Tailtiu*, the last queen of the Fir Bolg and the foster mother of *Lugh*, the Celtic warrior and champion. *Lugh* was the son of *Cian* of the Tuatha De Danann and *Eithniu*, the daughter of *Balor*, leader of the Fomorians. Their union was a dynastic marriage, following an alliance between former enemies, the Tuatha and the Fomorians. His father gave *Lugh* to *Tailtiu*, in fosterage, a common practice of the times that ensured peaceful relations between the two races. It was decreed that each year a festival of games should be held to commemorate the death of *Tailtiu*.

The festival became known as *Lughnasagh* and the games were similar to the ancient Olympic games and included athletic and sporting contests, trading of animals, the drawing-up of contracts, and matchmaking. Trial marriages were conducted, whereby young couples joined hands through a hole in a wooden door, a form of hand-fasting. The trial marriages lasted a year and a day, at which time they could be made permanent or broken without consequences. Another solemn ritual performed was the cutting of the first of the year's crops. After the cutting, some of it would be brought to the hill and ceremoniously buried. A meal of fresh corn and bilberries would then be made and everyone would partake. The Hill of *Tailtiu* was where the principal assemblies of the early *Uí Néill* dynasties were held.

Hill of Tara

In the center of the land taken by Tuathal from the province of Leinster, sat the Hill of Tara. The hill was first established as a place of sacred and political significance by the Tuatha De Dannan as early as 3500 BC. On the summit, with the Stone of Fal (stone of destiny,) as the focal point, sat the *Royal Enclosure*, a hilltop stronghold which was surrounded by an internal earthen ditch and further secured by a high, external bank. Within the confines of the structure, in addition to the dwelling houses, storage areas and stables, several important raths were built, the most significant being the *Royal Seat* and *Cormac's House*. Slightly north of the enclosure sat a passage tomb called the *Mound of the Hostages* and further north, a three banked ring-fort named the *Rath of the Synods*. To the south of the *Royal Enclosure* lay a ring-fort known as *Laoghaire's Fort*, named after one of Irelands high kings, Laoghaire mac Neill, who, according to legend, was buried there in an upright position. Farther north was the long, narrow rectangular feature known as the *Banqueting Hall* and nearby, three ring barrows, circular earthworks, known as the *Sloping Trenches* and *Gráinne's Fort*. Later, a roadway was constructed which linked Tara with *Eamainn Macha* (Navan Fort) in Co. Armagh, the royal seat of the kings of the northern province of Ulster.

With the amalgamation complete, Tuathal embarked on a program of restoration at Tara. A sturdy timber wall was installed around the site and the earthen ditches were deepened and strengthened. Watchtowers were erected and would be manned at all times, and heavy wooden gates, installed opposite the long, approach ramp ensured security for those inside. When the work was completed, Tuathal convened a general meeting during which it was decreed that a new province be named. The province of *Midhe* would henceforth be the dynastic center of Ireland where all future coronations, major royal and political decisions made and legal matters discussed. A *Feis* would be held every third year, soon after *Lughnasagh*, whereby new laws and customs would be instituted. Disputes over land ownership, inter-tribal squabbles and other petty crimes would be judged and settled by the Brehons (lawmakers) in court hearings, their decisions being final and absolute.

During the rebellion of 1798, United Irishmen formed a camp on Tara but were attacked and defeated by British troops on 26 May, 1798. Sometime later, the Stone of Fal was moved to mark the graves of the 400 rebels who died on the hill that day. In 1843, the Irish Member of Parliament Daniel O'Connell hosted a peaceful political demonstration on Tara in favor of repealing the Act of Union which drew over 750,000 people, and indicates the enduring importance of the Hill of Tara. During the turn of the 20th century the hill was vandalized by British Israelis who thought that the Irish were one of the Lost Tribes of Israel and that the hill contained the Ark of the Covenant.Tara today continues to impress and is included in the World Monument Fund's watch List of the 100 most endangered sites in the world.

3   The Destruction of Eamhain Mhacha.

According to both oral and written traditions, at the beginning of the 4th century AD, three brothers, known as the *Three Collas*, rebelled and killed their uncle, the high King of Ireland Fíacha Sroiptine. This singular barbarous act started a chain of fateful events that would have a devastating and far-reaching impact on the northern half of the island. After his uncle's death, his nephew, eldest brother Colla Uais, took Fíacha's kingship and ruled for three years (323-326 AD). He also laid claim to the overall kingship, and ruled as Ard Rí (high-king) of Ireland for four years. At the end of that time the murdered king's son, Muiredach Tirech banished the *Three Collas*, and exiled them and three hundred of their followers to Alba (Scotland).

The old annals of Tigernach tell us that the three brothers returned to Ireland, and traveled to Connaught where many of their relatives still lived. They approached the local King Muiredeach and with his help gathered a large army with the sole intention of raiding the province of Ulster. In 331 AD on the open plain of Farney, in what is modern day County Monaghan, a final, bloody battle was fought. The battle lasted for seven days and resulted in the death of Fergus Foga, the King of Ulster, and the routing of his armies. The royal seat at Eamhain Mhacha (Navan Fort,) the ancient capital of the province of Ulster, was burned down and destroyed. The victors then claimed the area as their own and re-named it Oirghíalla (Oriel.)

The name Oirghíalla means "the hostage givers" and the new kingdom was comprised of nine minor-kingdoms, each named after their ruling families. During its heyday, Oirghíalla ruled the modern dioceses of Armagh and Clogher, and controlled parts of counties Armagh, Monaghan, Louth, Fermanagh, Tyrone and Derry. Its main seats of power were the towns of

Armagh and Clogher. Oirghíalla stretched from Louth in the south to Derry in the north, and from Loch Neagh to Loch Erne. The new kingdom would last for almost a thousand years and go on to play a vital part in the history of the province of Ulster.

Another dynasty, the Uí Moccu Úais were composed of members of three tribes namely, the Uí Tuirtri, the Uí Maic Cairthinn and the Uí Fiachrach Arda Sratha, and were collectively known as the Uí Moccu Úais, eventually moved their bases to Counties Meath and Westmeath and near to the old kingdom of Brega.

The territory of the Oirghíalla from the 6th century onwards was gradually eroded by their neighbors, the northern Uí Néill, as well as the southern Uí Néill to their south. From 735 AD they were fully controlled by the Cenél nEógain, and by 827 AD had become their minions. The kingdom of Oirghíalla was at its zenith in the 12th century, under King Donnchad Ua Cerbaill. The later smaller kingdom of Airgíalla survived in Monaghan and was re-named Oriel after the Norman Invasion of Ireland. The kingdom of Oirghíalla came to a final end in 1585 when Rossa Boy MacMahon agreed to surrender and regrant his territories to the English Crown in Ireland, with his territory becoming County Monaghan in the Tudor Kingdom of Ireland.

Rossa Boy had ascended to the Oirghíalla kingship in 1579 and immediately found himself in an unfavorable position, wedged between an ever-expanding Tudor kingdom and Tír Eoghain under the control of the O'Neills. At first, he made overtures which suggested an alliance with Tír Eoghain, when he married the daughter of Hugh O'Neill, Earl of Tyrone. However, hoping to be left alone to run affairs locally, and after pledging allegiance to monarch Elizabeth I, MacMahon met with John Perrot, then Lord Deputy of Ireland, who according to some, was a natural son of the Tudor monarch Henry VIII, and agreed to join their Kingdom of Ireland. Oirghíalla, now known as Monaghan, was divided into five baronies under native Gaelic chiefs, mostly from the MacMahon clans.

This was not the end of the matter however because, fearful of the English moving in closer to his own lands, Hugh O'Neill turned to Brian Mac Hugh Og MacMahon of Dartree and married off another of his daughters to him. At the time, Brian Mac Hugh Og was the Tanist (leader) of his people according to the native Brehon laws and O'Neill was hoping to bring the Oirghíalla clans back to his side on the death of Rossa Boy through this agreement. For his part, Rossa Boy was trying to establish a pro-English succession through his brother Hugh Roe MacMahon. When the new Lord Deputy, William FitzWilliam began to pressure the acceptance of an English High Sheriff of Monaghan, O'Neill used his influence to exact opposition to it from clansmen in Monaghan, Leitrim, Fermanagh and Donegal. This prompted a military force led by Henry Bagenal, to be sent into the county in early 1589 to install the new sheriff and by the summer of that year, Rossa Boy McMahon was dead. In less than two decades all traces of the power of the Oirghíalla and the O'Neills would be consigned to the dusty pages of history.

Chapter 4
A New World Order

1   Christianity

Christianity, it is widely believed, had already taken a tentative foothold in Ireland before Saint Patrick arrived. Ciaran (the elder) had preached it in the late 4th century AD and was the first bishop of *Ossory* (Kilkenny.) In 430 AD Pope Celestine had sent a Bishop named Palladius to Ireland, whose mission was to minister to any that were already Christianized by that time. It has been speculated that an earlier form of Christianity may have been brought to Ireland by a warrior tribe called the *Attacotti*, in approximately 344 AD. In the 4th century AD it was commonplace for Irish raiding parties to strike settlements all along the coast of western Britain in the same way that the Saxons and Vikings would later attack Ireland.

Some of these raiders founded entirely new kingdoms in Scotland (*Pictland*) and, to a lesser degree, in parts of Cornwall, Wales, and Cumbria. The *Attacotti* are believed to have settled in the province of Leinster after arriving from Roman Gaul where, it is thought that they may have served in the Roman military in the mid-to-late 300s. They may have been exposed to early Christianity which was already making inroads in that region of France. In Ireland, Paganism, the main belief system at that time, was practiced by all of the Celtic tribes and ministered by a priest-like sect called Druids. These were the holy men of the Celtic peoples and commanded great respect among them but were seen as the stumbling block to the new religion.

2   Ireland and the Desert Monks

Christian monasticism, which would greatly influence Ireland's unique form of Christianity, developed in Egypt between the 2nd and 3rd centuries AD, with most of the ascetics during that period of history living solitary lives in simple huts or caves and were called hermits. An ascetic named Anthony, who was born around 250 AD, had decided to retreat from society and devote himself to a solitary, contemplative life. After his parents died, he gave away his inheritance and went to live in an abandoned fort in the desert located between the Nile and the Red sea, and for twenty years saw no other human. Soon, others inspired by his lifestyle became followers and set up simple stone shelters around the fort, which later became known as 'cells.' Anthony's followers kept him supplied by throwing bundles of food and goatskins filled with water, over the walls of the fort.

One of those followers, a man named Pachomius, was born in Thebes, modern day Luxor, in 292 AD to pagan parents. He was drafted into the Roman army against his will, at age 20 and held captive. He wrote that local Christians, at great risk to themselves, brought food and water to the captives and these acts of kindness made a lasting impression on him. For Pachomius, that was the spark and when he was finally released he sought out one of Anthony's ardent disciples, the hermit Palaemon, and became his follower. Pachomius later took the next logical step and grouped the small 'cells' into a formal organization and in this way the first monastery was born. Pachomius knew instinctively that oral knowledge could easily be lost and so insisted his followers become fully literate. This would ensure that as much information as possible could be saved if written down. Pachomius was hailed as Abba which means father, and from this we get the word Abbot.

I feel that it is important now, to write a little about the invaluable role the female followers played during this period. While perhaps not as well remembered as their male counterparts, they are nevertheless, a vital part of this story as without their support and equal dedication, it is unlikely that the work of the males would have been as successful as it has been.

Mary, Pachomius' sister, had lived in a cave near to him and gathered, over time, a group of other women who became the first, all female monastics. These women were adept at illustrating manuscripts as well as drawing detailed sketches for the architects who would eventually build the monasteries. They also wove the tapestries that adorned the walls and made the exquisite robes worn by the clergy. Reading and writing were taught by these women as well as many forms of art.

Basil the Great was born in Cappadocia around 330 AD into a wealthy and influential family. He is arguably the most influential of the Greek monks and was greatly influenced by his sister Macrina. As a young man Basil had desired to become a lawyer but was persuaded by Macrina, to follow a more spiritual path. After a visit to Egypt he decided to found his own monastery and went on to write 'The Monastic Rule' which is still adhered to by the Greek and Slavonic churches today.

Brigid is arguably the most influential of the Irish female monastics. She was born in County Louth. Ireland in 453 A.D. Her father is believed to have been a pagan Chieftain of Leinster and her mother a Christian *Pict* and slave whom St. Patrick had baptized. She built a small oratory in County Kildare which was a center of religion and learning that eventually became a Cathedral city. She also founded two monastic institutions, one for men and the other for women. She also founded a school of art, including illumination, metalwork and a scriptorium.

3   Ireland and Egypt.

In A.D. 451, the new Byzantine Emperor Marcian, an orthodox Christian, ordered a new Ecumenical council be convened to establish once and for all, the belief that Christ was and is both God and Man. Pope Leo 1 called for it to be held in Italy but Marcian insisted it be held in Nicea.

Unfortunately, Attila the Hun, who was not a Christian, orthodox or otherwise, was on the rampage at the same time. This prompted the organizers of the Council to relocate to Chalcedon, an ancient maritime town situated on a peninsula near the Bosphorus, opposite the old city of Byzantium. The main aim of the new council was to set aside the findings of the Second Council of Ephesus, held in 449 AD and which had become known as the 'Robber Council.' The Council of Chalcedon issued the 'Chalcedonian Definition' refuting earlier beliefs that Christ was solely a God. The council bishops declared that Christ has two natures, God and Man. The Council's decree is not accepted by large numbers of monks and the ancient Eastern Churches, including the Orthodox of Egypt, Syria, Armenia, Eritrea, and Ethiopia. A major schism occurred soon after the Council ended, that lingers to the present time. Out of the ashes of the Council of Chalcedon arose the Orthodox Christian sect who chose the Church of Alexandra as their spiritual leader. These monks cut their remaining ties with the Church of Rome, retreated back to their desert bases, and indeed, many more actually fled from Egypt at this time.

In 2006 the discovery of an ancient book in a bog in County Tipperary, Ireland, sparked an exciting debate. The book, Egyptian in style and with pages made of papyrus, lends credence to an ancient story which tells of a visit to Ireland by 'seven monks of Egypt.' In an early 'Litany of Irish Liturgy,' *Oengas of Tallaght*, mentions the burial of seven Egyptian monks in County Antrim. Another early literary source, the 'Stowe Missal' (c750) mentions the desert monks and in particular, Anthony of Egypt. There is a manuscript, written sometime in the 8th century and kept in the British Library (Nero A11), London, which puts forth the theory that the desert monks of Egypt greatly influenced the behavior and lifestyles of the Irish monks. Author and historian, Archdale King, writes that "firsthand knowledge of the Desert monks was brought to southern Gaul by St. John Cassian and that links between the Irish and Egyptian monks were particularly strong at this time." King also mentions an *Ogham* inscription on a stone near Saint Olan's well in the parish of Aghabulloge, County Cork, which has been interpreted as reading "Pray for Olan the Egyptian."

Much of the contact between Egypt and the British Isles took place before the Muslim Conquest of 640 AD. There is evidence of a trade route through the Mediterranean and in a passage of the life of St. John the

Almsgiver, the Greek Patriarch of Egypt, reference is made to "a vessel sailing from Britain to Alexandria bearing a cargo of tin." This tin most likely came from Cornwall or Somerset, well known areas of Britain for tin mining. An Irish monk named *Dicuil*, in his 'Liber de Mensure' written in 825 AD, describes the pyramids in great detail as well as an early version of the Suez Canal leading us to believe that visits were often made to Egypt by pilgrims on their way to the Holy Land.

The 'Saltair Na Rann,' an anthology of biblical poems attributed to *Oengus the Culdee*, also contains the 'Book of Adam and Eve,' and was composed in Egypt in either the 6th or 7th century AD, and is known in no other country except Ireland. It is believed that the Irish monks, inspired by the lifestyles of the desert monks, sought out similar places in Ireland as their retreats. While there are no actual deserts in Ireland, there are places which afforded desert-like qualities, places that were remote and away from the everyday hustle and bustle. One notable example of this can be seen on the windswept island of Skellig Michael, a monastic settlement that sits about 11 kilometers west of the Iveragh peninsula in County Kerry, 600 feet above the wild Atlantic Ocean, and which was hewn from the bare rock by Irish monks in the 6th century AD. As a matter of note, the word Disert or Dysart (solitary place) appears in many Irish place names.

4   The Scribes

In A.D. 406 during a particularly harsh winter, the river Rhine froze over. Across this temporary land bridge poured hordes of Germanic tribes led by the charismatic Aleric, King of the Visigoths. This singular event precipitated the fall of the Roman Empire and the dark ages began with a vengeance. With the fall, Europe descended into chaos and darkness, all scholarship ceased, books were burned and learned men were rounded up, imprisoned and executed, the blackboard was being erased. Ireland being an insular island escaped all of this mayhem and actually blossomed intellectually during this period due in large part to the foresight, dedication and tenacity of a handful of scholar monks. Those brave men travelled far and wide across the then, known world, and collected as much of the written history that had not already been destroyed. They brought the written words back to Ireland and passed them on to their brothers, the scribes.

I can, if I close my eyes and it is very still, conjure up the vision of a monk alone in his cold, stone cell, isolated in a dark monastery, the silence shrouding him as he pored over those ancient scrolls by candlelight, his eyes bright with wonder. Then, word for word, reveal, translate and transcribe with a quill he fashioned from a reed, or perhaps a goose feather and ink that he himself mixed. In the deep silence you would hear the scratch of the nib as he wrote on the stiff parchment and for him, at that time, it must have been a sacred and painstaking task. It amazes me when I think of the time, patience and dedication those men had in order to ensure that future generations would come to know and marvel at their revelations. For the most part, they were of good cheer and never lost their sense of humor. If you look closely at any of their works, you will notice, in the margins, their scribbled jokes, usually at the expense of a fellow scribe

5   Pagan High King Laoghaire

In 431 AD and three days after the festival of Lughnasagh, a lone figure stood, head bowed in contemplation, next to one of five carefully positioned chairs, in the Great Assembly Hall at Tara in the province of *Royal Midhe* (Meath.) Four of the chairs, laid out to mirror the points of the compass, faced the fifth chair which sat directly in the center of the hall. The seat, with intricately carved arm rests and a high-back, was adorned with inlaid ivory, fashioned from the tusks of a wild boar. The hall, part of a sprawling, fortified hilltop complex constructed on an east-west axis, three hundred feet long, thirty feet high, sixty feet wide, had fourteen doors and on that occasion, waited in patient silence in readiness for the important gathering scheduled to take place later in the afternoon. Several other large buildings erected around the Great hall included residences for each of four provincial kings, a large smoke house, where all food was prepared, a house for holding the hostages belonging to the high king, a house for the Brehons and Bards and a house, the *grianan na nInghean*, for the wives, children and servants of the provincial kings. Together with its stables, storehouses and warrior's quarters, all surrounded by deep earthen ditches and earthworks, and reinforced by a solid wooden palisade, made Tara a secure, imposing stronghold which dominated the landscape and could be seen from many miles distant.

The sole occupant of the Great Hall on that day was no ordinary mortal and anyone observing him would have been struck by his stature and regal mien. Long haired, full bearded and standing almost six feet tall, his long sleeved *leine* (tunic) fashioned by skilled weavers from gleaned flax plants, was colored bright red and reached down well below his knees. A broad leather *crios* (belt) circled his waist, held his wand of office, a dagger, a small pouch and helped keep his *leine* in place. His four folded, richly embroidered woolen *brat* (cloak) had the five colors of the nobility, was trimmed with fox fur, reached almost to the floor and pinned with an ornate golden broach at his right shoulder. Around his neck hung the gold *nasc niadh* (chain of valor) that he had inherited from his father, signifying his status as a warrior. His hand stitched sandals, tanned from the soft hide of a fallow deer were dyed purple, denoting his rank, wrapped around his ankles and were held together with strings of leather.

Laoghaire Mac Neill, whose journey to the kingship of Ireland would follow a convoluted and unorthodox path, was a younger son of the celebrated late 4th century warrior King Niall. From the beginning of his reign in 379 AD, Niall had set out on a campaign of subjugation, starting in the southern province of Munster. He soon overwhelmed the other three provinces in quick succession and then led raids against the Britons, Picts, Saxons and Dalriads. His imposing army, comprised of Irish, Scoti, Picts, and Britons, crossed the English Channel and proceeded to Brittany where they fought and defeated the *Morini* tribe. As was the custom after each victory, tribute, including livestock and hostages, were taken and returned to Ireland with the conquering army. Among the many captives taken during the raids in Britain, Alba (Scotland) and France was a sixteen-year-old Roman boy named Patricius, (who would ironically have a long and far reaching effect on Ireland and its people later in the 5th century.) When the hostages were eventually apportioned, Patricius, by then the property of a local Chieftain and druid named *Milchu*, went north to the province of Ulster where he became a sheep-herder on the slopes of Slemish, an extinct volcanic mountain in County Antrim. After six years in captivity, he managed to escape and traveled across country to Killala bay, County Mayo where he boarded a ship bound for Britain and eventually re-united with his family.

Niall of the Nine Hostages, as he became known, led his last military campaign in France in an effort to free a local Celtic tribe from Roman oppression. As he and his army were encamped on the banks of the river Liane near the commune of Boulogne-Sur-Mer, an archer in Niall's army, a vengeful son of *Eochaidh*, the King of Leinster, shot an arrow which pierced Niall's heart, killing him instantly. The bad blood between *Eochaidh* and Niall arose when *Eochaidh* attempted to illegally claim the kingship of Ireland. After a brief skirmish, Niall routed the pretender and banished him and his followers to Alba (Scotland.) On the death of Niall, a son of *Fiachra* named *Dathi* was crowned as King and ruled Ireland until his death from a bolt of lightning while on a military campaign in the French Alps. *Dathi* has the distinction of being the last pagan king of Ireland before the coming of Christianity. After his death, Ireland was once again without a king and the road to Tara was opened for Laoghaire.

In 428 AD, after a reading of the 'Instruction for Kings,' written many centuries earlier by the high King Cormac, and in which was inscribed a summary of the customs and laws of the country, Laoghaire Mac Neill was presented with the white *slat na ríghe* (rod of kingship) during a joyous coronation ceremony held at the stone of Fal on the hill of Tara. The white rod, usually cut from a rowan tree, chosen specifically for its color and straightness, was blemish free and signified truth, justice and integrity. Attending the coronation were the four provincial Kings, all their wives and children, Nobles, Brehons (judges) ard Ollams (scribes) Harpists, Bards, chief Druids (priests) and Chieftains. When the coronation ceremony ended, Laoghaire would be known as *Ard Rí* (high king) of all Ireland. Everyone returned to Tara in August 431 AD as requested, to attend and participate in the *Feis* (assembly) which Laoghaire had convened. The *Feis of Tara*, one of three general assemblies held in Ireland, included the *Feis of Eamhain*, in the province of Ulster and the *Feis of Cruachain*, in the province of Connaught. Both of those assemblies were primarily concerned with choosing master craftsmen, including Blacksmiths, Woodworkers and Stoneworkers who, when selected, were sent to each of the provinces to do their work. The more important *Feis of Tara*, held every third year, was an official assembly of the leading men of the whole island and not a meeting of all classes of society. Its constitution and place of meeting were fixed, and the times of meeting regular. The primary purpose of the *Feis of Tara* was the reaffirmation of national unity and security, but among the other duties performed was the establishment of new laws and customs. Any disputes regarding title to rank, property and privilege would be settled by the lawmakers, the Brehons, and all annals and records would be carefully noted and entered by the Ard Ollams in the official records. Any previous law, custom or record not included, was deemed to be false and irrelevant, and as Laoghaire stood waiting in the hall, all of these matters were of great concern to him knowing as he did that his decisions would have long lasting and far reaching effects on the country. But on that day, another more serious development weighed heavily on his mind, compounding the already tense situation.

6   High Druid Lochra

*"A tailcenn (*baldhead*) will come over the raging sea, with his perforated garments, his crook-headed staff, with his table (altar) at the east end of his house, and all the people will answer 'Amen! Amen!"*

Soon after Laoghaires' ascension to the throne, *Lochra,* Laoghaires' trusted chief Druid, beset with feelings of unease and worrisome thoughts, began to have a frightening, recurring dream. In the dream, he was naked and tied to a large, white oak tree, the last one standing. The symbols of his birthright and power, his inscribed stones of divination and his oft-used staff, lay scattered and broken on the ground at his feet. All across the land the sacred oak groves had been cut down and burned on large pyres and the hilltop fortress of Tara was gone. In its place on the hill above the wide valley, he could see a high, wooden cross, silhouetted against the backdrop of the western sky. A strange man, holding a staff with a crooked top, appeared to be addressing a large crowd, was calling his name and with outstretched arms, beckoned him to join them. The dream worried *Lochra* and he knew that it was only a matter of time until it's meaning became clear to him.

With a lineage stretching back through several generations, *Lochra* held the secrets and rituals of divination which had been passed down orally to him through the years. Starting when a young boy, he had been taught, first by his grandfather, and later his father, in all aspects of foreseeing the future and when he was deemed to be proficient, was given the staff of knowledge, cut from the old growth of a Rowan tree, the symbol of his power. His first responsibility as advisor to the new king, was to accurately foretell any and all events that may have an impact during the time of the king's reign. *Lochra*, fully aware of the importance of his position within the royal household, took his duties seriously. Until now, he had successfully guided the people in all things; the best time to plant crops, when to reap, what herbs to use to cure illness. He was the teacher and knew all and when they had doubts and fears he reassured them, without him they would be lost. But recently, rumors were spreading of a foreigner landing on their shores to the north, speaking in a peculiar language about new things and *Lochra* had heard that he had gone to a rowan tree and cut a staff from it. He knew of this stranger and understood he would have to face him soon, and even though he did not fear the violent legions in the lands to the east, this lone figure scared him with his other worldly knowledge.

Earlier in the year, on a warm summer afternoon, *Lochra* took his leave of the royal house, walked slowly down the earthen ramp and followed the well-worn path to the sacred oak grove. After entering, the quiet and coolness surrounded and comforted him as he made his way toward the cave in the center of the circle of white oaks. Within the sacred circle, he chanted the spells of clarity, touched each tree with his staff and spread ashes from the recent *Lughnasadh* fire at their bases. He then rested on a flat rock at the mouth of the black cave, deep in thought, his purple robes and long white cloak fastened about his neck with a golden clasp. His long hair and beard were silvery as a moon's glow and neatly combed. His brow, deeply etched, spoke of the many years of worry endured on behalf of his beloved people, but his bright blue eyes were clear and focused. His sturdy staff leaned against a moss-covered rock by his side and as he sat, he read again the old *Ogham* inscriptions which were cut into the outer cave wall. He had added his own over the years, using a sharpened piece of flint. The carvings always gave him inspiration in times of doubt, and he had doubts now. So many relied on him alone that his broad shoulders sagged as he worried about what was to come.

He always entered the silent realm when vital decisions had to be made, and as he pondered, the veil slowly parted and he was granted a vision. With piercing clarity, he could see a robed figure standing on a pebbled beach, on the northern shore, a crooked staff in his right hand. A deep sense of foreboding swept over *Lochra* then, like a cold ocean wave, and soon he was awash with dark, dreadful thoughts of self-doubt and insecurity. This man had come, not with an army but with symbols more powerful. What was he to do? He had heard that the man had been here once before as a boy, taken by a raiding party from his home in the land to the east and had lived as a sheep herder on the slopes of the fiery mountain. But that was many years ago, and the boy had since returned to his own people across the sea. Now he had come back. Why? What did it mean?

In commune with his ancestors, he reached into the deerskin pouch that hung about his waist and brought out the inscribed stones and small animal bones from within. They had been passed down to him by his father many years ago, and as he shook them in his loosely cupped hands, he chanted the spells that would invoke the wisdom of the ancients, and cast them on the ground. Bending over to read, he noticed the dark eyed, dappled fawn emerge from the cool forest, and after passing through a patch of fading sunlight, approach him unafraid. This was an omen and not unusual, and as she came closer and nestled at his feet, he reached out to her, as if to greet an old friend. As he stroked the silken fur on her breast, gently, she licked his hand. At that moment, a wren lit on the branches of a small blackthorn tree nearby, and sang her song for him. He smiled then knowing what he must do. Another glance at the stones confirmed his belief, and picking them up, returned them safely to their resting place. He then rose to go back to his people, tell them of his revelations and fulfill his destiny.

On his arrival back at Tara, *Lochra* requested and was granted a private meeting with King Laoghaire. At the meeting, he told Laoghaire of the vision he had had while on his sojourn and prophesied that, "a *tailcenn* (baldhead) will come over the raging sea, with his perforated garments, his crook-headed staff, with his table (altar) at the east end of his house, and all the people will answer 'Amen! Amen!'" *Lochra's* prophecy came to pass soon after and he advised Laoghaire to be wary of the *tailcenn* as he was a threat to their time-honored customs and way of life. Agents were dispatched with instructions to closely observe the stranger and report his movements and practices. Word had come back to Tara, via messengers, telling of a man, whom the people were calling Patricius, and his retinue who were traversing the country speaking to them about a new God who had sent his son to the earth to save them. He told them that they must forsake their old Gods and beliefs, their custom of animal sacrifice, their worship of trees and that they must embrace the new way of life or be dammed forever in everlasting fire.

Many, including Laoghaire's daughters *Eithne* and *Fedelm* had already embraced Patricius and agreed to the new philosophy and Laoghaire, fearing for the future, had ordered his death. Two separate attempts were made on his life, but he somehow managed to survive each one. It was further reported to Laoghaire that Patricius had erected a house and shrine at *Ard Macha* and another one at Cashel where people were meeting and worshiping the new God. It was also reported to Laoghaire that *Aonghus*, the King of Connaught and *Daire*, the King of Ulster, had welcomed Patricius and invited him to their royal residences where they had accepted the new faith and were baptized. When news reached Tara that Patricius had lit a fire on the Hill of Slane during the spring equinox, Laoghaire was infuriated. The law was specific and stated that 'no other spring fires be lit except for the festival fire at Tara.' Fearful, desperate, and under increasing pressure, Laoghaire demanded that the troublemaker attend the *Feis* at Tara and explain his intentions to the assembly, if he refused to attend, he was to be brought before the King by force.

7 The Feis at Tara

In the Great hall, the attendees had begun to arrive and take their seats. King Laoghaire, already seated in his royal chair in the middle of the hall, was surrounded by his ten hand-picked individuals who attended him at all times and included a "high ranking Nobleman to be his companion; a Brehon judge to deliver and explain the laws of the country in the King's presence upon all occasions; an antiquary or historiographer to declare and preserve the genealogies, acts, and occurrences of the nobility and gentry from time to time as occasion required; a chief Druid or Magician to offer sacrifice, and presage good or bad omens, as his learning, skill, or knowledge would enable him; a Bard to praise or dispraise every one according to his good or bad actions; a physician to administer physic to the king and queen, and to the rest of the royal family; a musician to compose music, and sing pleasant sonnets in the King's presence and three Stewards to govern the King's House in all things." The King of Munster sat in the chair facing south; the King of Leinster sat facing east; the King of Connaught sat facing west and the King of Ulster sat facing North. Their Nobles, Chieftains, Druids and attendants were seated behind their respective kings and the Ard Ollams had their own special seating area close to the east wall.

At the time appointed, the master of ceremonies, the *Seanchas*, stood facing the king and at a given signal, declared the Feis to be in session. After delivering the welcome address, Laoghaire called for the Roll of Kings to be amended to include his name, rank and genealogy. The chief judge (brehon) wearing the *Iodhain morain* (collar of truth) then declared the Roll to be legally binding and ordered it be entered in the annals for posterity. Next, the royal physician was called upon and declared the King to be of sound mind and body and fit to rule. Each provincial king, in his turn, wearing the *lodhain morain*, was then called to give a detailed account of the affairs of his province including any disputes, criminal activity, infractions and outstanding *eiric* (tribute) not yet paid. Punishments including fines, forfeiture and banishment, set by the panel of judges, were imposed and made binding by royal decree. The amount of yearly *eiric* from all provinces, payable to the king, was decided upon and distribution of hostages finalized. The *Ollamhs* made careful and accurate note of all the events that transpired and inscribed them, word for word in the official records. The final issue not yet resolved was the matter concerning the troublemaker Patricius and King Laoghaire dispatched two of his stewards with orders to bring him before the court.

Positioned between the Great hall and the mound of the hostages, sat the dwelling where Laoghaire's wife Queen Angias, her children, attendants and servants were housed. Built in similar style to the other houses it was smaller than the Great hall but bigger by half than the other structures. With three doors and a large well-fueled open hearth, it was warm, welcoming and comfortably furnished. Colorful banners and woolen wall hangings adorned the wooden walls and helped insulate the hall against the coming Autumn chill. A long trestle table was laid out in readiness for the expected visitor and when summoned, servants would bring platters of food, fresh baked bread, fruit, jugs of mead and honey and wine made from the berries of the elder tree. Queen Angias, the daughter of *Ailill Tassach*, a former King of Munster, seated between her two daughters and holding her son and heir *Lughaidh* on her knee, waited patiently for her guest to arrive.

She was looking forward to the visit and remembered her daughters telling of their first meeting with the man called Patricius at the sacred site of *Cruachain* in the province of Connaught. *Eithne* and *Fidelm* had arrived home visibly excited and in awe of the teachings of the man. They told of how he had used the *uisce* (water) from the well to wash away their sins and how he had cast new powerful spells over their heads and how he had spoken to them of a wonderful place called paradise. Angias, aware that increasing numbers of people, including the Kings of Connaught and Ulster, together with many Nobles and Chieftains, had already received Patricius and been baptized by him, knew that sweeping changes had begun. With wisdom, as befitted her lineage, she was sure that fundamental change was inevitable and while she understood her husband's turmoil and had had many discussions with him on the matter, she had encouraged him to embrace the new ways.

8   Patricius the Roman

"Could I have come to Ireland without thought of God, merely in my own interest? Who was it made me come? For here I am a prisoner of the Spirit so that I may not see any of my family. Can it be out of the kindness of my heart that I carry out such a labor of mercy on a people who once captured me when they wrecked my father's house and carried off his servants? For by descent I was a freeman, born of a Decurion father; yet I have sold this nobility of mine, I am not ashamed, nor do I regret that it might have meant some advantage to others. In short, I am a slave in Christ to this faraway people for the indescribable glory of everlasting life which is in Jesus Christ our Lord."

Patricius, from his letter to the Soldiers of Croticus.

In 403 AD, Patricius (Patrick) a young Roman boy of sixteen was taken hostage, together with his sisters *Lupida* and *Darerca*, by a raiding Celtic army led by the Irish warrior King Niall. Following a series of raids throughout Alba (Scotland) and Britain, Niall's army, together with their hostages, crossed the English Channel and proceeded to Brittany in France where they fought with a tribe called the *Morini*. In France, Patricius became separated from his sisters and was brought to Ireland by the returning army.

He was sold to a wealthy chieftain/druid named *Milchu* and traveled north to the province of Ulster where he became a sheep-herder on the slopes of Slemish, an extinct volcanic mountain in County Antrim. By his own account, for six years he lived a lonely life and wrote about his experiences later, in two letters that have survived. After his years in captivity, he managed to escape and traveled across country to Killala bay, County Mayo where he boarded a ship bound for Britain and eventually re-united with his family.

Patricius was born in Nemptor (Dumbarton) a citizen of the Roman Empire, in 387 AD. His father Calpornius, was a deacon, his mother was the sister of Martin of Tours in France and his grandfather Potitus, a priest. Religion was in his blood and soon after his return to his family he was sent to Auxerre, France to study religion and theology. It is known that he spent several years at Marmoutier Abbey in Tours, France and was eventually ordained as a bishop by Germanus of Auxerre at Lérins Abbey. At his own request, Patricius was sent to Ireland in approximately 430 AD shortly after his appointment as a missionary, by Pope Celestine, where Christianity, it is widely believed, had already taken a foothold. A tribe named the *Attacotti* are believed to have settled in the province of Leinster after arriving from Roman Gaul where, it is thought that they may have served in the Roman military in the mid-to-late 300s. They would have been exposed to early Christianity which was already making inroads in that region of France. A monk called *Ciaran* (the elder) had preached it in the late 4th Century AD and was the first bishop of *Ossory* (Kilkenny.) Earlier, Pope Celestine, had sent a Bishop named Palladius to Ireland to minister to any that were already Christianized by that time, and had some success. Patricius, when he arrived, would have had many contacts already Christianized from which he could draw on for support. Coupled with the financial backing of the wealthy church of Rome, all made it unlikely that he would fail in his mission.During his six years as sheep herder in County Antrim, Patricius acquired a good knowledge of the Celtic language and a broad understanding of local customs, all of which would be a great benefit to him during his mission of conversion. After several years of missionary work among the *Morini* people in France, Patricius eventually set sail for Ireland. Failing to land in County Wicklow, due to the hostility of the local population, Patricius and his followers sailed up the east coast and landed at a small island off the coast of Skerries, Dublin. After a short respite, they continued to sail north and landed safely at the mouth of Strangford Lough, near to the modern-day town of Downpatrick. A local Chieftain named Dichu gave him a small piece of land in the townland of Saul, near Strangford Lough in County Down on which Patricius built his first shrine. His first act as the new representative of the church of Rome, was the ordination of Bishops and priests and the baptism of as many of the local populace as possible. His simple message of salvation appealed to many and converts flocked to him everywhere he went. By his own admission, Patricius admits that he used bribes among the Nobles and Brehons in exchange for the freedom to travel unmolested around the country.

In the last week of July 431 AD, Patricius left his residence at *Ard Mhacha* and traveled with his retinue south toward the kingdom of *Midhe*. He had been summoned, by royal decree, to a meeting with the reigning monarch, King Laoghaire Mac Neill at the court at Tara. His journey would take him along the *slige midluachra* (royal roadway) that wound from Antrim on the north coast, through *Eamhain Mhacha*, the seat of the kings of Ulster, through the foothills of Slieve Gullion and the gap of the north, passing near to the hamlet of Dundalk, on past the old, moss covered dolmens and burial place of the nobles at *Ros na ri*, on through the town of Drogheda and over the hill of Slane. Then, after crossing the river Boyne, arrive at the royal residence at Tara where he would stay overnight as a guest of Queen Angias and attend the *Feis* on the following day. Despite the earlier attempts on his life, Patricius was unafraid and eager to meet with Laoghaire. Although acutely aware of his connection to Laoghaire's father Niall and his time as a hostage in Ireland, Patricius believed that fate had brought him full circle and was sure that his meeting with Niall's son was inevitable and the final hurdle to be cleared.

As he walked along, he let his mind wander, back to the fateful day when the wild, pagan marauders attacked his village and family home, burning and looting with impunity. He recalled his mother and father shouting at him and his sisters, urging them to run and hide and the fear and panic as the young men and girls, including him and his sisters, were rounded up and taken to the boats. He remembered his time as a shepherd, tending to the sheep and goats on the rugged granite crags of the cold, wet mountain and the absolute loneliness surrounding him like a burial shroud, sustained only by his unwavering faith. He shivered as he thought of the stormy nights when the howling wind roared and the thunder rocked the very ground where he lay trembling in abject fear. He could still feel the crackle of electricity on his skin as he thought of the night sky ablaze with fiery light, the furze and bracken lit with an eerie, hellish glow, each flash etched in his memory forever. He recalled how he had prayed earnestly every day imploring God to free him from his bondage and allow him to return safely to his family. By God's grace he had survived it all; intimidation, threats of imprisonment, death and banishment, but he was aware that there was still considerable opposition to him and his new message, even though he had converted many among the nobles and other important people. High King Laoghaire and *Lochra*, the chief Druid, his main opponents, were the real stumbling block and he knew that unless he converted them, his mission could falter.

Patricius arrived at Tara in the early evening and was escorted to the royal residence by the gatekeepers, where Queen Angias and her daughters waited to welcome him. Already a convert, she and her daughters had looked forward to his arrival and after exchanging pleasantries, led him directly to the seat reserved for him at the head of the table. Among the guests were *Aonghus*, the King of Connaught, *Daire*, the King of Ulster, *Benignus*, son of the chieftain *Secsnen*, who would later become Patricius' successor and *Erc*, the son of the important noble *Daig*, who would later become the Bishop of Slane. All had been baptized and converted to the new faith, were loyal followers of Patricius and would accompany him to the meeting with Laoghaire the next day. Despite the seriousness of the scheduled meeting, everyone was in good spirits and enjoying the food, hospitality and quiet conversation when a sudden, anguished cry startled everyone at the table.

On the floor, near to the open hearth, *Lughaidh*, the four-year-old son of Laoghaire and Angias, lay motionless. His elder sister, *Lupida* was bent over him and seeing that he was gasping for air, looked around, her eyes wide with fear and called again for help. Angias jumped to her feet and ran to where her son lay lifeless and fell on her knees. Picking him up, she ran to the table and implored Patricius to save him. Holding the small, lifeless body in his arms, Patricius could see that the child was not breathing, even though his mouth was wide open. Peering closely, he noticed something lodged in the child's throat, obstructing the airway. Placing *Lughaidh* on the table, Patricius, praying aloud for guidance, reached his fingers into the boy's mouth and removed the obstruction, a piece of un-chewed meat, and miraculously, the child began gasping for air and started to breathe normally.

Handing the frightened child to his mother, Patricius told her that her son had been saved by the power of Michael the Archangel. Relieved and overjoyed, Angias assured Patricius of her eternal gratitude and devotion, promising to do all in her power to promote him and his message of salvation. Later that night, when the guests had retired and were asleep, Angias told Laoghaire of the miracle that had occurred earlier in the evening and was eager to convince him that if not for Patricius' rapid intercession their son would surely have died. She urged him to listen to what Patricius had to say and even if not completely in agreement with his message, at least allow him to preach to those who wanted to listen.

Patricius arose before dawn the following morning and after a light breakfast of oatmeal and water, walked the short distance to the highest point on the hill. There, beside the ancient stone of Fal he would be able to see for miles in all directions, and as he watched, the first rays of sunlight crept slowly across the landscape, bathing the hills, valleys and the meandering river below, in a glorious morning glow. He marveled as the crisp, autumn air was warmed, causing the early mists to evaporate and smiled as it's heat caressed his upturned face. Looking north, he could see a herd of small, red deer quietly grazing on the still shaded, dew covered, grassy slopes of Slane, the hill where he had lit the fire that had incensed Laoghaire earlier in the spring. Toward the eastern horizon, on a hill above the river, he could see the old, stone burial mound, held sacred by the Druids, and where he and his followers had argued with *Lochra* and the Brehons, one of many encounters that had come to blows. As time passed, he sat in the mid-day sun and reflected on his long, arduous journey, which began all those years ago, praying that today, it would all come together as divinely planned. He then rose and made his way back to the Queens house and as he neared the entrance, two of Laoghaires stewards approached him and told him the King was waiting and that he must go with them. Patricius, together with *Aonghus, Daire, Benignus, Erc* and three priests bade farewell to Angias and walked the short distance to the great assembly hall and entered.

Inside, a silent, stern-faced audience watched as Patricius walked to the center of the hall, stood at the recommended distance and faced Laoghaire across the wide floor. At a table, close to the north wall, the Brehons sat, dressed in their yellow robes; the *Ollamhs*, seated near to the east wall, their writing materials neatly laid out on the table before them in readiness for inscription of the events. The *Seanchas*, ordered that the charges be read and the chief Brehon rose, unfurled a parchment and began to read aloud the charges levelled against Patricius:

1   *That he promoted worship of an alien God in defiance of the King's decree.*

2   *That he accepted gifts from wealthy women and converts.*

3   *That he accepted payment for performing baptisms and ordinations.*

4   *That he gave gifts to Nobles and judges in return for land and property.*

Turning to face the Brehons, Patricius began to speak:

"As for our God, He is the God of all men. He is God of heaven and earth, of sea and rivers; He is the God of sun and moon; of all the stars. He is the God of the lofty mountains and of the lowly valleys. God, above the heaven and in the heaven and under the heaven, has His dwelling around heaven and earth and sea and all that in them is. He inspires all things; He quickens all things; He transcends all things; He sustains all things. He gives its light to the sun; He veils the light and knowledge of the night. He made fountains in the parched land, and dry islands in the midst of the sea; and He appointed the stars to serve the greater lights. He has a Son, co-eternal with Himself and co-equal with Himself. The Son is not younger than the Father, nor the Father older than the Son; and the Holy Spirit breathes in them; nor are Father, Son, and Holy Spirit divided. I wish to unite you to the heavenly King, our savior, inasmuch as you are the children of an earthly king and must be baptized. Amen."

Continuing his address, he further stated that yes, he had accepted small tokens of appreciation from grateful patrons, but had since returned them. He told the judges that he did not accept payment for baptisms, nor for ordaining priests, and indeed he personally paid for many gifts to kings and judges, and paid for the sons of chiefs to accompany him on his mission. Any properties on which he built shrines and small churches, had been either given to him freely as donations or purchased by him personally. He was prepared to do whatever he deemed necessary to save their mortal souls, it was his pre-destined duty to do so. He reminded the gathering that two kings and many Chieftains' sons, including *Benin*, the son of the powerful chieftain *Secsnen*, had joined Patricius group and more were flocking to the group in large numbers every day. His mission included baptizing thousands of people, ordaining priests to lead the new Christian communities, converting many wealthy women, some of whom became nuns in the face of family opposition and interacting with the sons of kings, converting them too. He was prepared to give his life for his beliefs and those who continued to worship the false gods and refused baptism, would be lost forever. Having spoken honestly as required, guided by his faith, he had answered the charges brought against him, and without further comment, Patricius then turned, motioned to his companions, and together they walked out of the great hall.

The annals tell us that, faced with overwhelming numbers who had converted, coupled with pressure from at least two of the provincial kings and members of his own family, Laoghaire did indeed allow Patricius to continue his mission untroubled. The saving of his son's life would have greatly influenced his final decision and it is recorded that Laoghaire agreed to baptism by Patricius, making him the first Christian King of Ireland. After his conversion, the Code of the Laws of Ireland, known as the Seanchas Mor, was drawn up. King Laoghaire reigned as Ard ri of all Ireland from 428 AD to 463 AD and was buried in an upright position at Tara, according to his father Niall's decree. His son Lughaidh went on to become high king after his father's death, the only one of his sons to do so. Queen Angias, so grateful for the miracle that saved her son's life, promised to give a sheep out of every flock she possessed each year and a portion of every meal she should take during her lifetime to the poor in honor of Michael the Archangel. She established it as a custom throughout Ireland for all who received baptism. The custom is still adhered to today and is known as the 'Michaelmas sheep' and 'Michael's portion,' celebrated on September 29, as Michaelmas Day.

It is worth mentioning that Patricius went on to become the most revered figure in Irish Christianity and continued to convert and baptize people all across the island until his death in 461 AD at the site of the first shrine he established at Saul in County Down. He lies at rest together with Brigid and Colmcille under a large stone slab in the nearby churchyard.

Chapter 5
Battles and Raiders

1   The Battle of the Book

In early Christian Ireland, the old Druidic tradition collapsed due to the spread of the Christian faith. The study and learning of Latin, coupled with the new Christian theology in monasteries, was flourishing. In 561 A.D., a seminal event occurred that would have a profound and long lasting effect on Irish Christianity, spark a war, divide two major monastic seats of learning, and forever change the lives of all involved.

On a frigid, mist shrouded morning in 563 AD a battered, wave tossed *curragh* (boat) came to rest on the rocky shore of the island of Iona, known as the 'Isle of Hermits,' just below the ruins of an old, iron age fort. The tattered leather sail and thin wicker sides, covered in cracked and split cow hides, attested to the dangers encountered by anyone brave or desperate enough to challenge the open ocean. Nevertheless, on that day, the soaked, shivering crew of thirteen men had little choice as their lives were at stake. Expelled from Ireland, their homeland, in the wake of a violent war which claimed more than three thousand lives, they had to flee under threat of death, never to live again in the land of their birth. Their meager possessions, prized books and writing materials, a few saintly relics and a gold altar cross, had thankfully survived the treacherous journey. Ironically, the cause of their exile was an argument over a single book.

Two centuries earlier In 347 AD, a man whose writings would change the Christian world, was born at a place called Stridon, a small village that straddled the border of Dalmatia, in north-eastern Italy. The son of Eusebius the bishop of Caesarea, Jerome was an historian, theologian and like his father before him, a translator. His translations of the original Hebrew biblical writings into Latin, became known as 'Jerome's Vulgate,' a comprehensive work and the earliest version of our modern day bible. 'Jerome's Vulgate' would go on to have a profound and long lasting effect on Irish Christianity and forever change the lives of all involved. Later in 495 AD, a scholar monk and scribe named Finnian, sometimes referred to as 'Finbarr the white head,' (a reference to the color of his hair,) was born in the north-east of Ireland in the province of Ulster. He founded a monastic settlement overlooking Strangford Lough, in an area that today we know as County Down. Attached to the monastery was a school and scriptorium, which became a renowned center of scholarship, learning and translation. Movilla Abbey, (monastery of the plain of the notable tree,) taught all subjects including mathematics, geography, history, language and religion. Built on the site of an earlier pre-Christian, Druidic place of learning, it may have taken its name from a local forested area covered with large trees, which were sacred to the ancients.

Traveler monks and scribes regularly left the monastery and scoured the then known world, seeking knowledge and inspiration. On their return, perhaps years later, they passed on to their fellow scribes, all materials that they had garnered, most of which was written in the language of its country of origin, notably Greek, and Hebrew. Undaunted, and with their otherworldly abilities, the scribes painstakingly pored over the ancient writings and converted them to the Latin and Gaelic languages. Eager pupils from all over Ireland came to Movilla to study and learn the craft of translating and illuminating manuscripts. One of the pupils who enrolled in the school was a scholar named Colmcille, also known as Columba, who was described as "a striking figure of great stature and powerful build, with a loud, melodious voice which could be heard from one hilltop to another."

Colmcille was born in 521 AD in Gartan, modern day County Donegal, Ireland. He was the great-great grandson of Niall of the Nine Hostages, an Irish high king who reigned in the 5th century. As a teenager he enrolled in the school at Movilla, and studied under the abbot Finnian.

By the age of twenty-one he was already a deacon and with his studies completed, he travelled south to Leinster and became a pupil of an old bard named Gemman. His studies with Gemman complete, he then entered the monastery of Clonard, situated on the River Boyne in modern day County Meath. During that period, many of the important names in the history of Irish Christianity studied there, the average number of scholars sometimes exceeding three thousand. Another of Colmcille's teachers was the esteemed scholar monk, Mobhi, whose monastery at Glasnevin taught such famous men as Ciaran, Canice and Comgall, many of whom would later become known as the Apostles of Ireland.

In 540 AD, on his return to Ireland from a trip to Rome, Finnian had in his possession a copy of the book, 'Jerome's Vulgate.' Knowing that he had in his hands, a vitally important work, his intention was to translate, transcribe it into the Gaelic language, and distribute among the many monasteries and schools. Unbeknownst to Finnian, Colmcille, his brightest pupil, had borrowed the book without his knowledge and did his own translation, with the same intentions as Finnian. Finnian, enraged, demanded Colmcille return the copy, but was met with an unwavering refusal. This incident sparked the confrontation that became known as the 'Battle of Cúl Dreimhne' (Battle of the Book,) which took place at Cairbre Drom Cliabh (County Sligo,) in 561 AD.

"To every cow belongs her calf, therefore to every book belongs its copy."

King Diarmait mac Cerbaill.

That quote, in essence, conveyed the King's decision in regard to what was essentially the first copyright case ever brought before an Irish court and perhaps the world. Finnian, whose loyalty and fealty was to King Diarmait, petitioned him to intervene in the dispute. A hearing was duly convened and lawyers for both parties argued their client's respective cases. Finnian's side argued that as he owned the original manuscript, he also owned the copy. Colmcille's lawyers, while agreeing to Finnian's ownership of the original, disagreed with the King's decision regarding the copy, and argued that as Colmcille did all the work of translating and transcribing, the copy should be his. Nonetheless, the King's word was final and the matter appeared to be settled. But this was not the first time the King had incurred Colmcille's ire and for him, it was the last straw. Soon after, he set out to avenge the wrongful decisions. The first event that had so incensed Colmcille, occurred earlier, probably in 560 AD, when Curnan of Conn Acht, a relative of Colmcille, fatally injured a member of an opposing team during a hurling match. Fearing for his life he sought, and was granted refuge with Colmcille. King Diarmait sent several of his heavily armed men to arrest Curnan and after a violent struggle, dragged him from Colmcille's arms and killed him. That act was a blatant defiance of the age old Law of Sanctuary and prompted Colmcille to enlist the aid of the O'Neill clan and urge them to rise up and do battle with King Diarmait.

Early one fateful morning in 561 AD on a verdant, open plain, in what is now County Sligo, both armies assembled, faced each other across the wide expanse, and prepared to go to war. Nothing could stop it, not even the intervention of respected *Filid* (bards) with their words of appeasement. The die was cast, and now blood would stain the furrows and bracken as far as the horizon. At days' end, almost three thousand men lay dead and dying in mortal agony, their death throes, haunting, pitiful screams, resounded on the soft evening air and could be heard on Tara, some miles distant. The blood soaked shields and broken *claidebs* (swords) lay scattered all around, some still clasped tightly in the hands of the butchered, broken bodies of the vanquished. That night, a pall of deathly silence enveloped the sorrowful plain, and nothing stirred for days.

Later, when the horror had subsided and sanity returned, a Synod of clerics and scholars was convened. Some of those who attended the Synod blamed Colmcille solely for the deaths and called for his execution, some favored excommunication, but when Brendan of Birr, a noted theologian, spoke on his behalf, a deal was made that allowed for the option of exile instead. Colmcille's conscience troubled him so badly he sought the advice of an elderly Hermit named Molaise. After much careful consideration, Molaise advised Colmcille to do his penance and accept the offer of exile. Colmcille duly left Ireland, and returned only once, many years later.

Finnian's monastery went on to become a very successful seat of learning and scholars having heard of his teachings and sanctity, flocked to the monastic retreat. The traditions taught at Movilla were based on the scriptures contained in 'Jerome's Vulgate,' but also used the practices of the Desert monks of Egypt. Colmcille founded an important abbey on Iona, which became a dominant religious and political institution in the region for centuries. He was highly regarded by both the Gaels of Dál Riata and the Picts, and is remembered today as a Christian saint and one of the Twelve Apostles of Ireland. Although in exile, he remained active in Irish politics, though he spent most of the remainder of his life in Scotland. What remains of his copy of 'Jerome's Vulgate,' is housed in the Royal Irish Academy in Dublin.

2   Return of an Exile.

On a cold, wet evening in 576 AD a flotilla of small, wave tossed, leather covered boats with tattered cloth sails, came to rest on the rocky shores of Lough Foyle close to the modern-day town of Limavady in what is now Co. Derry, Ireland. Upon reaching the safety of the shoreline those on board, gave thanks and praise for their safe deliverance from the wild, frigid waters of the North Atlantic Ocean, and made their way inland. Having started out from the small island of Iona in the Outer Hebrides, the boats, joined together for safety with hand woven hemp ropes, had followed close to the rugged coastline of Scotland and then navigated south-west toward the mouth of the river Foyle, Ireland. On board were a retinue of twenty bishops, forty priests, fifty deacons, and thirty students of divinity.

Their leader, the noted scholar Colmcille, who was banished from Ireland many years earlier for his role in a violent confrontation that became known as the "Battle of the Book," had been ordered, as punishment, to never again return to or set eyes on the land of his birth. Colmcille duly left Ireland with twelve followers and settled on the windswept Isle of Iona, in the Western isles of Scotland. He built a monastery there in 563 AD which eventually became a noted seat of learning throughout the continent of Europe. Colmcille, a brilliant teacher and theologian, was also a lover of the arts and earnestly promoted all artistic endeavors, particularly the oral traditions. Although in exile, he kept abreast of the political and religious affairs and events in Ireland and was consulted on many occasions as an advisor. Being a distant relative of Aedh

(Hugh) the reigning King of Ulster, Colmcille didn't hesitate when invited to attend an important convention decreed by King Hugh's royal mandate.

In 576 King Hugh convened the "Convention of Dromceat' and summoned the chieftains, princes, nobles and religious leaders of the kingdom with instructions to meet at the royal enclosure on the flat-topped mound of Dromceat, just south of the modern-day town of Limavady in Co. Derry. The reason for the convention was three-fold and the issues to be debated were; the expulsion of the *Filid*, the tribute owed the King by the Dailriads of Scotland, which, if not resolved would result in an armed invasion, and lastly, the removal by the King of Scanlan Mor as the rightful King of Ossory, Kilkenny. Hopefully, by the end of the discussions, the issues would be resolved to the satisfaction of all parties involved.

From the beginning of his reign King Hugh found himself in an unenviable position and under increasing pressure from many factions countrywide regarding the role played by the *Filid* within the Irish nobility. The issue was not a new one, it was a problem that he had inherited from the time of Connor Mac Neasa, the former King of Ulster, who reigned many years before Hugh came to the throne, and was passed down through the reigns of two other kings of Ulster, Fiachadh and Maolchabha, finally arriving on Hugh's doorstep. The dispute centered around the ever-increasing number of *Filid* who, it was widely believed, were abusing their power and positions of privilege among the nobility, for personal gain. The word *Filid* comes from the same root as the Welsh word meaning "to see" and is a collective term given to all Ollamhs, Bards and Poets.

It is believed that originally, *Filid* were all powerful, holding high office as magicians, lawgivers, judges, advisors to the kings, composers and poets. They were made up of a large, aristocratic class and as professional poets, could and did command payment. Some charged large fees for their services and made good use of what was known as the 'Poet's curse' to ensure their continued power and employment. It was firmly believed that a well composed verse could ruin a person's reputation and cause harm and even hasten the death of an individual. Of course, as with all matters pertaining to the human condition, some *Filid* overstepped the boundaries and were taken to task for their infractions.

Considering that *Filid* enjoyed a privileged existence with their day to day living expenses and their accommodations paid for by their employers, the nobility, it's easy to understand that many individuals would aspire to join their ranks. During King Hugh's time, there were more than twelve hundred Ollamhs, Bards and poets widely dispersed throughout the entire kingdom of Ireland. This would doubtless put a strain on the coffers of their employers and as in any society, would have surely caused a rise in *eiric* (taxation.) Something had to be done. Over the years, several attempts had been made to remove, or at least reduce the number of Ollamhs, Bards and poets in the country. Many had voted for their banishment to Scotland, but each time this was proposed, the reigning King of Ulster had intervened on their behalf and granted them sanctuary.

At Dromceat, double, high-banked earthen ditches, topped with a sturdy wooden palisade encircled the mound and lookouts were posted at intervals along the length of the walls. Within the confines were several well-maintained structures including a large hall for meetings, accommodations for visiting dignitaries, storehouses, stables, quarters for the king's bodyguards and set off to one side and facing east, sat the king's private residence. The site had been carefully chosen as a meeting place for several important reasons; it offered a commanding view of the surrounding countryside was easily defended and most importantly, was situated in neutral territory. Neutral territory was important in this instance as king Hugh had ongoing local disputes that had to be settled regarding the political and military relationship between the King of the Dalriads, Aedan mac Gabrain, who owned land in the north of Ireland and the west of Scotland and the powerful northern Irish overking Aed mac Ainmirech from Donegal. Hugh's intervention would hopefully resolve the situation and thus avoid any violent confrontations.

In Geoffrey Keating's "History of Ireland" there is an account of the meeting that took place between King Hugh and Colmcille. Colmcille, besides being a great scholar, was also a clever politician and he requested a private audience with King Hugh. Out of a healthy respect for Colmcille's' reputation as a man not to be trifled with, permission was granted and the meeting took place in the King's private residence on the eve of the Convention and was quite informal. An onlooker could not have failed to notice the stark differences between the two men. Hugh, long haired, full bearded and close to six feet tall, wore the six colors of the nobility. Colmcille, broad shouldered and of similar height, was clean shaven and whose carefully tonsured hair was cut short and neatly combed, wore the long brown, woolen habit denoting his stature as a man of God. After exchanging the required pleasantries of formal introduction, King Hugh invited Colmcille to speak.

Colmcille, asking the King's favor, told Hugh that he had three requests to propose, which, if they were granted, he would be convinced that the 'civility and reverence showed him outwardly by the King was real and undisguised.' Hugh, afraid to disoblige, replied, that 'whatever his petitions were, if it was in his power, they would assuredly be granted.' Colmcille then asked that Hugh 'retract his banishment of the *Filid*, and to not send them out of the kingdom: that he should release Scanlan Mor from incarceration and reinstate him as rightful King of Ossory: and that he should not send his army into Scotland, to raise the *eiric*, rents and contributions of the Dailriads, or to raise their tribute beyond what was paid to his predecessors.' The King answered that 'It would be of infinite prejudice to his government to give any protection to the poets, for they were a lazy, covetous, and insatiable body, and an insupportable grievance to the people ; that their numbers increased daily, every superior poet taking state upon himself, being followed by a retinue of thirty, and those of a lower order retaining a proportionate number of attendants suitable to their several degrees, so that a third part of the whole kingdom had entered themselves into the society of the poets, to the great decay of trade and industry, and the senseless impoverishment of the country. Therefore he was obliged, for the ease of his subjects, and his own safety, to purge the island of them, and transplant them into new settlements.'

Colmcille patiently listened to the king's reasonings, and convinced by the force of his argument replied that, 'it was indeed necessary that the Bardic schools and houses of learning should be reformed but not suppressed; that he, Colmcille, would consent to a reduction of their numbers, but that it would be a wise idea if his majesty, retained a poet of honesty and distinction in his court to preserve the history, exploits and record the genealogy of his family and allow all other provincial kings and nobles to do likewise.' This proposal was accepted by Hugh and the expulsion of the poets was prevented, and this regulation was the standard by which the society of poets were directed in future ages. This agreement between Colmcille and King Hugh is recalled in the words of the poet called Maolruthuin who wrote:

"The poets were saved from banishment by Colmcille who, by his sage advice, softened the king's resentment, and prevailed. So that every Irish monarch should retain a learned poet; every provincial prince, and every lord of a cantred, were by right allowed the same privilege and honor.'

From this agreement between Hugh, the King of Ireland, and Colmcille arose the continued custom that 'every Irish monarch must employ and maintain a learned and accomplished poet in his court. Every provincial prince and lord of a cantred must do likewise, and were obliged to settle a fixed salary upon their poets, sufficient to afford them an honorable maintenance, and secure them from the contempt of the people.' A new system of apprenticeship was established whereby all *Filid* had to devote as many as twelve years of their lives to studying and learning and by the end of the apprenticeship would have memorized more than three hundred different meters, at least two hundred main stories and about one hundred lesser stories. The apprenticeship employed the use of sensory deprivation and the novice would spend long periods of time alone in a dark cell with nothing but his own mind for company. It was believed that in this way only, could the higher realm be accessed, the place where all inspiration emanates. When his learning period was complete, the *Filid* was only then allowed to wear the coveted 'cloak of crimson bird feathers' and carry a wand of office.

From then forth, the *Filid* would be held in high esteem, and their patrimonies and properties inviolable. In public wars and commotions, they were exempted from plundering and contributions, they paid no taxes or acknowledgments to the state, and their houses were invested with the privilege of a sanctuary, and not to be forced without sacrilege and impiety. There were colleges erected, and large revenues settled upon them, where learning and arts were taught and encouraged. Rath Ceannaid was an academy in those times and so were Masruidh and Maigh Sleachta in Breifne. Free schools were opened, and youth educated and instructed in antiquity, history, poetry, and other branches of valuable and polite learning.

Colmcille's second request that of the release of Scanlan Mor and his re-instatement as King of Ossory was denied, which displeased him so much that he told the king that 'Scanlan should be released, and that very night should untie the strings of his brogues at the time when he was offering up his midnight devotion, or a terrible curse would befall the king.' The third favor that Colmcille had asked of the king that he would not send his army into Scotland to raise the tribute and taxes that were usually paid by the tribe of the Dailriads, 'for it would be an encroachment upon their ancient privileges, and contrary to the established laws of his predecessors, to commit hostilities upon that honorable clan, which was always ready to assist the Irish crown with their arms, and expose their lives with great bravery in its defence' had no effect upon the king, who resolved to invade Scotland with a powerful army and compel that tribe to gratify his demand. Colmcille answered that 'providence had taken that illustrious clan into its peculiar protection, which was able and resolved to set bounds to the tyranny and exactions of the Irish crown, and would deliver the Dailriads from so unjust and unprecedented oppressions.' With nothing left to discuss, Colmcille took leave of King Hugh and summoning his retinue, left Dromceat and prepared for their return to Iona.

3   The Destruction of Royal Brega

Ask most people who they believe were the first group of foreigners to launch highly organized, violent raids in Ireland, and they will usually say it was the Vikings, who raided Lambay Island in 795 AD. What many people are not aware of is that a century before the emergence of the Vikings, an equally violent group, not from the Fjords of Norway, but from a place much closer to home, beat them to it.

On a cold, wet morning in the year 686 AD, a determined individual set sail from a, jagged, windswept island, nestled on the westernmost edge of the Inner Hebrides. His long, hazardous journey would take him down the rugged west coastline of Scotland and then inland to the kingdom of Northumbria. If he survived the dangerous trek, he planned to enter negotiations with King Egfrid, (a Saxon), and arrange for the release of sixty men, women, and children who had been taken as hostages from Ireland two years earlier. The man's name was Adomnan, the abbot of a monastery on the small isle of Iona, founded by the Irish scholar monk Colmcille in 563 AD. Colmcille had been expelled from Ireland as a result of his involvement in the 'Battle of Cul Dreimhne' and he, along with twelve followers went into exile on Iona and built a monastery there. The monastery was hugely successful, and would play a vital part in the religious conversion of the Picts during the late 6th century and of the Anglo-Saxons in 635 AD. Iona went on to take its place as one of the most important monastic centers in Europe.

In the 7th century the islands of Ireland, Britain and Scotland were made up of a series of conflicting dynasties and warring kingdoms. It was not uncommon for a king, who felt that he was all powerful, to invade his neighbors and demand fealty. In Anglo-Saxon England the most powerful kingdom was Northumbria, ruled by the ruthless King Egfrid. The Kingdom of Northumbria was a medieval kingdom in what is now northern England and south-east Scotland and was reportedly founded by a Saxon leader named Ethelfrith. Ethelfrith, it is believed, defeated the armies of the Britons in approximately 600 AD at the Battle of *Catraeth* (Catterick.) The Britons gave him the name *Flesaur*, which translates to "the twister." The *Saxons*, a Germanic tribe that lived close to the North Sea coast of what is now Germany, amalgamated with another, equally ruthless tribe known as the *Angles* and immediately started to raid their neighbors. As raiders and vicious plunderers, they were perfectly positioned geographically to send raiding parties to ravage the British Isles. Significant numbers of them settled in large areas of Great Britain in the early Middle Ages and formed part of a group known as the *Anglo-Saxons*. Eventually, they became the dominant force and formed what we know today as the United Kingdom.

In the Leap year 684 AD, a disciplined and well-armed military force, commanded by King Egfrids' top *ealdorman* Berht, sailed out from their settlements on the western edge of Northumbria and made way for a staging post on the Isle of Man. Like their counterparts the Vikings, who would follow their lead a century later, the *Anglo-Saxons* had death, plunder and pillage on their collective mind. The target on that night was the royal Irish kingdom of *Brega* at *Midhe* (Meath) the seat of Irish power. Their oft used methods were highly successful, had always worked perfectly in the past and would be no different this time either. Move fast, use the night shroud of darkness to surprise, unearthly noise to scare and bewilder, and the sword and axe to subdue. Spare no-one, save the hostages, as they could be used as barter later on.

The name *Brega* translates as the 'fair plain,' a reference to the large, wide, fertile expanse of land that today straddles the modern counties of Louth, Meath and Dublin. To the east of *Brega* lay the Irish Sea and to the south, the River Liffey. The kingdom ran all the way north across the *Bru na Boinne* (Boyne Valley,) and stretched as far north as the mountains in Louth. The King of *Brega* at that time was Fínsnechta Fledach mac Dunchada. The term *fledach* was added to his name as a tribute to the personality of the new king and means "the bountiful." He had been crowned as the King of *Brega* and also as the *Ard Ri* (high king) of Ireland, on the nearby Hill of Tara. Two important supporters of his were the King of *Fir Rois* and the abbot Adomnan. He belonged to a branch of the southern O'Neill clan, an important dynasty whose descendants ruled Ireland until their defeat in the nine-years' war of 1603.

When they were sated, the invaders retreated; in their wake, a bare, devastated wasteland as far as the horizon. Smoke from still smoldering fires in the fields and storehouses hung heavy on the air, choking and stinging the eyes of the few remaining survivors. Butchered corpses of both human and animal lay strewn in grotesque indifference where they fell, the royal enclosure breached, sacked and burned, was left in ruin. The headless corpses of the nobles, mutilated in a frenzied orgy of bloodlust, silenced; the royal lifeforce seeping into the earth. The church and monastery, which once sang the praises of both king and creator, reduced to piles of scorched, scattered stones, forlorn. The houses, usually filled with love, laughter and joyous celebration, now razed with violent hatred, a pitiful sight. Everything of value, including surviving livestock, religious artifacts and hostages, the women and children, were then dragged to the *Saxon* ships for transport to Northumbria.

The Anglo-Saxon Chronicle entry for that year stated that "churches were attacked and burned," and names the *Saxon* commander in the field as the *ealdorman* Berht. The 'Venerable Bede,' a scholar monk and author, from the kingdom of Northumbria, called the attack "an unwarranted attack on innocent, Christian people," and criticizes Egfrid, King of Northumbria, who planned and authorized the raid. Bede goes on to tell how clerics, including the *Saxon* bishop Egbert, repeatedly warned against such actions and that "God would punish the *Saxon* king for such a terrible act." Abbot Adomnan 's trek was ultimately a success, and he returned the hostages safely back to their families. In 688 AD Fínsnechta abdicated his throne to become a monk, but left the clerical life and resumed the kingship in 689 AD.

4   The Vikings

Toward the end of the 8th century AD, Ireland was almost completely Gaelic and Christian. It was a rural society with no towns or cities and the only large settlements were hamlets that grew up around Monasteries. The Monastery was firstly, the seat of learning but was also involved in the cultural, economic and political affairs of its province.

On a crisp, calm morning in 795 AD, a flotilla of longships slipped their moorings at a staging post, hidden deep within a cragged fjord in Norway. On board, companies of well-armed, disciplined marauders, intent on conquering and plundering new lands. Many of those sailing that day were the younger sons of nobles and warriors who, because of a rapid rise in population and subsequent shortage of land; compounded by their low ranking within their families, were forced to seek elsewhere. Expert boat builders, they constructed the longship with precise attention to detail, speed being the main, determining factor. Ideally suited for open sea voyages, it was lightweight, lay low in the water, had a wide beam, and was fast and stable. Fitted with oars as long as the boat itself and with cloth sails, woven from sheep's wool, all ensured that they could increase speed when needed, and supplement the rower's efforts. The low draft allowed navigation in shallow waters, making it ideal for river travel, and made rapid beaching possible. With both bow and stern built identically, they could reverse direction without having to turn. Expertly trained navigators among the crews of the long ships, used the sun, moon and stars as guides. The sunstone, shadow board and a rudimentary form of compass, made certain that they reached their chosen destinations.

Sailing out from the fjord, they tacked southwest, skirted the Shetlands, and sailed south to Orkney. After a short respite there, they continued down the Atlantic Ocean, hugging the coast of Scotland, bypassed the isle of man and directed the convoy toward the land that lay furthest from the then known civilization. Their target on this day was a small monastic settlement on Lambay Island, which lay two miles off shore, close to *Dubh Linn* (Dublin) a marshy area at the mouth of the River Liffey, Ireland. The settlement, built in 530 AD, by an Irish scholar monk named Colmcille, was home to a handful of monks and scribes. A church, monastery and several small, corbelled stone huts and simple shelters were built close to the site of an ancient stone-axe quarry. Rocks from the quarry were hewn by the monks, dressed by hand and utilized as the building material for the dwellings. Living a spartan existence, the monks possessed little and the only items of value were the books, religious artifacts and holy relics that adorned the church and monastery walls.

The Norsemen, better known today as the Vikings, had their own religion and worshiped a pantheon of Norse gods, some of whom promoted violence as a means to an end. They detested Christianity and saw it as a direct threat to their way of life and everything they held dear. That is one reason why they targeted monasteries and churches with such frequency, although they did also raid the houses of noblemen and isolated farms. Another attraction, and perhaps the deciding factor, was that the monasteries contained many gold and silver ornaments of worship. They also knew that the inhabitants of those settlements were god fearing and peace loving individuals, unarmed and less likely to struggle. After looting the artifacts and relics, the settlement was destroyed in an unbridled orgy of destruction, the buildings reduced to piles of smoldering rubble. The naked bodies of monks lay butchered, grotesquely strewn on the ground where they fell. Those not slaughtered were rounded up and shackled in readiness for transport back to the fjords, and their new lives as slaves.

5   The Battle of Tara

"Every one of the Gaeidhil who is in the territory of the foreigners, in servitude and bondage, let him go to his own territory in peace and happiness."

Those words, uttered in 980 AD by the powerful Máel Sechnaill mac Domnaill, the O'Neill King of the Royal Kingdom of *Midhe* (otherwise known as Malachy II,) spelled the beginning of the end for the Viking rulers of Dublin. The first raid on Irish territory by the Vikings was the destruction of a small monastic settlement on Lambay island, which lay two miles off shore, close to *Dubh Linn* (Dublin,) a marshy tide pool at the mouth of the River Liffey, Ireland. That first raid was the beginning of two hundred years of intermittent warfare and pillage with monasteries the favored targets, but these raiders spared no-one. They were expelled from Dublin in 902 AD but remained active in the Irish sea where they continued to raid the Pictish kingdom in Scotland, the *Saxon* kingdom in Northumbria and frequently ravaged Manx. They returned to Ireland in 914 AD, where they landed a large fleet of Longships in Waterford and proceeded to raid and plunder countrywide, with a vengeance.

The Viking city of Dublin had by the 10th century grown into a wealthy and powerful trading center and part of its wealth was based on the export and sale of Irish slaves who were captured in periodic raiding expeditions. But by the end of the 10th century the power of the Vikings was beginning to wane as the Irish Kings became more powerful. In 980 AD, Malachy II defeated the Vikings of Dublin and their allies from the Hebrides and the Isle of Man in a decisive battle at Tara in Co. Meath. The battle of Tara led to the abdication of *Sitric*, the Viking ruler of Dublin, and his banishment to the monastery of Iona. The battle lead to the accession of Malachy II to the High Kingship of Ireland and the defeat of the Viking army opened the way to Dublin.

The Annals of the Four Masters record that the following year Malachy advanced on Dublin and following a siege of three days, captured the city. He then released over 2,000 hostages held by the Vikings and forced them to renounce the tribute they had exacted from the O'Neills. Then he issued a proclamation freeing all the Irish slaves in the territory of the Vikings. The freeing of the slaves and curtailment of further slaving would have had an impact on the wealth and power of the Dublin Vikings and make them less of a threat in the future. No doubt the freeing of the slaves could be seen as a calculated political move to make Malachy popular throughout Ireland, but it can also be seen as a display of humanity from a medieval warrior King. Malachy would remain High King of Ireland for another 22 years when he was succeeded by Brian Boru who would also fight a famous battle against the Vikings of Dublin at Clontarf in 1014.

Chapter 6
Invaders and Plagues

1   The Normans

The dispossession of Diarmait Mac Murchada, the High King of Leinster, from his lands by the High King of Connaught, Ruari O'Connor, eventually led to the ouster of many of the old Gaelic families from their lands and the start of serious hardship and wars that continue to the present day. To recover his kingdom, Mac Murchada enlisted the aid of Henry II of England. Mac Murchada left Ireland in 1166 and travelled via Bristol, England to Aquitaine, France, where he met with Henry II. Henry could not help him at that time but gave him an open letter of introduction. He was eventually and some would say fatefully, granted a meeting with Richard de Clare, one of Henry's top aides. This noble character was the son of Gilbert de Clare, the first Earl of Pembroke. Richard, affectionately known as 'Strongbow,' was out of favor with Henry II at that time for taking King Stephen's side in a battle against Henry's mother, the Empress Matilda. Because of his treachery, Richard couldn't inherit his father's title, but nevertheless endowed himself with the name Strongbow. Richard de Clare and Diarmait Mac Murchada met in 1168. A deal was struck between these two upright citizens whereby for De Clare's assistance with an army, he would be given the hand of Aoife, Mac Murchada's eldest daughter. More importantly, Richard would be in line for the Kingship of Leinster through marriage.

An army was assembled which included companies of Welsh and Flemish archers, revered for their skill with the longbow. This invasion army was led by Raymond FitzGerald and in quick succession it overwhelmed the Viking established towns of Wexford, Waterford and Dublin in 1169-1170. Strongbow did not take part in these battles and only arrived in Ireland when the dust had settled, in late 1170. In 1171, Mac Murchada died and his son Donal claimed the Kingship under the ancient Brehon Laws but Strongbow was having none of that and he claimed the Kingship as his right by marriage. Soon after, Ruari O'Connor led an army against Strongbow but was driven back in a series of violent battles after which O'Connor and the remains of his army retreated to Galway. Meanwhile, Henry, back in England began to get worried about the success Strongbow was having and decided to invade Ireland himself. This he did in 1172 and claimed the title, Lord of Ireland and Richard was stripped of his title at that time. Henry II signed the Treaty of Windsor in 1175 and under the terms, Ruari O'Connor was granted the Kingdom of Ireland, minus Leinster, Meath, Dublin and Waterford. Ignoring the terms of the treaty, Strongbow invaded Connaught in 1177, but was severely defeated by O'Connor in an epic battle. Many of the old Gaelic families were stripped of their lands and titles around this time and one of the lasting effects of this invasion by Henry II was Anglicization of many of the old Gaelic names.

The Normans, now ensconced in all four provinces, initiated a policy of widespread castle building. Their well protected strongholds, they hoped, would ensure complete control over the native population. But like all other invaders before and since, they failed to understand the undaunted and indomitable spirit of the Irish. The Irish noblemen planned insurrection and enlisted the aid of a group of like-minded individuals from Scotland.

2   The Gallowglass

The Gallowglass, as they were called, were elite mercenary warriors and members of the Gaelic clans of Scotland. As Gaels, they shared a common background and language with the Irish, but as they had intermarried with the Vikings, the Irish Gaels nicknamed them *Gall Gaeil* meaning *foreign Gaels*. Large numbers of gallowglass settled in Ireland after losing their land and property during the Scottish Independence wars. Many of the Irish Chieftains gave them shelter and land in exchange for their promise of future military service. The gallowglass were a well-trained, well-armed and disciplined infantry and had always proven themselves to be strong defenders of their positions, and utterly fearless. In battle they used the two handed sparth axe, a claymore, several throwing spears and at least one dagger. Each warrior had two young squires in attendance to carry provisions and maintain weapons. They wore iron helmets and body armor that consisted of chain mail on top of heavy, padded jackets. The Gallowglass formed in groups of one hundred men called *Corrughadh,* similar to the system employed by the Roman legions.

With the aid of companies of Gallowglass, an uprising in 1261 defeated the Normans in Kerry. In 1270 the O'Connor clan routed the Normans from Connaught. In 1274 Wicklow had also been recaptured and by 1300 many areas of the country were once again in the hands of the Irish noblemen. In 1296, the Norman king, Edward 1st of England, in an unprecedented move, invaded Scotland. After a series of violent and savage battles, his armies took control and eventually ruled Scotland for ten years. Edward further incurred the wrath of the Scottish people when he removed and brought the 'Stone of Scone' back to England. The ancient stone, the seat and symbol of Scottish power, was used in the coronation ceremonies of all Scottish kings, and considered a treasure of the Scottish Royal family. It was kept by England for seven hundred years and only returned in 1996. The theft of the 'Stone of Scone' was the last straw and set in motion a plot to regain Scottish independence.

3   Edward Bruce

In 1306, a Scottish chieftain named Robert Bruce plotted to overthrow the Normans and regain Scottish independence. With the aid of several Scottish lords and their many associated clans, Robert Bruce defeated them at the battle of Bannockburn in 1314 and soon after, was crowned King of Scotland. In the province of Ulster, Ireland, two powerful clans, the O'Neills and O'Donnells, were heartened by this victory in Scotland and sent emissaries to speak to Robert Bruce in hopes of enlisting his aid in defeating the Normans that remained in Ireland. A deal was struck in which the king's brother, Edward Bruce would be crowned *Ard Rí* (high king) of Ireland, in return for their assistance.

In 1315 a large, disciplined army led by Edward Bruce, landed at Larne in Ulster, just north of Belfast, County Antrim. They marched south to the royal kingdom of Meath, and after a bloody battle, defeated the Norman forces. In May 1316 Edward was crowned King of Ireland and later that year his brother Robert Bruce arrived in Ireland with his considerable forces. The brothers, with their combined armies, marched on the Normans of Limerick, Tipperary and Kilkenny, routed them and destroyed their property. Robert returned to Scotland leaving Edward to complete the removal of the remaining Normans.

4   The Famine of 1315

The Great Famine of 1315–1322 was the first in a series of large-scale disasters that devastated the continent of Europe in the 14th century. The Famine began with heavy rains in the spring 1315 causing crop failures all across Europe which didn't recover until late in 1322. The crisis brought extreme levels of crime, disease, millions of deaths and even cannibalism. The disaster had major consequences for the Church, state and European society as a whole. In 1317, Ireland was seriously affected by the Famine with a shortage of food and provisions. People had to revert to being hunters and gatherers and began to collect wild roots, hazelnuts, acorns, plants, grasses, and tree bark in the forests. Because of the lack of food for his troops, Edward Bruce's military campaign was severely hampered during this time and slowed their advance. This, just when it seemed that finally, the Normans would be ousted from Ireland for good. In October 1318, Edward marched north to County Louth where he engaged a large Norman army. North of the town of Dundalk, at the battle of *Faughart*, County Louth, Edward's army was defeated and he died from his wounds some time later. Despite this setback however, Norman control of Ireland was being methodically eroded.

5   William de Burgh

William de Burgh (Burke) the 3rd Earl of Ulster, was born on 17 September 1312. He was the son of John de Burgh and Elizabeth de Clare. He married Lady Matilda of Lancaster, daughter of Henry Plantagenet, 3rd Earl of Lancaster. In 1332, at Greencastle, Donegal, close to the shores of Lough Foyle, he had his cousin Sir Walter de Burgh murdered by means of starvation. In revenge, Sir Walter's sister, Gylle de Burgh, wife of Sir Richard de Mandeville, planned his assassination. In 1333, William de Burgh was assassinated by Richard de Mandeville, Sir John de Logan, and others. The Annals of the Four Masters noted that "William Burke, Earl of Ulster, was killed by the English of Ulster. Those responsible were put to death, in divers ways, by the people of the King of England; some were hanged, others killed, and others torn asunder, in revenge of his death."

This single act had a profound and long lasting effect on Irish affairs and the struggle for independence from England. After his death, de Burgh's lands were divided among his relatives which resulted in a split with the Norman leadership in Dublin and started what became known as the Burke Civil War. After changing their name, the Burkes of Connaught rebelled against the English crown and proclaimed themselves to be solely Irish. This meant that all lands west of the River Shannon were now under Irish control. In the northern province of Ulster, the O'Neill clan took power and in 1364 they became the Kings of Ulster. Burke's only daughter Elizabeth, Duchess of Ulster, married Lionel of Antwerp, third son of Edward III of England.

6   The Bubonic Plague

A silent, unseen killer, born on the arid plains of Central Asia, attached itself to the rampaging Mongol armies, and traveled with them purposefully, along the Silk Road, arriving in the Crimea in 1343. The killer then boarded the myriad of merchant ships that plied the waters of the Mediterranean and spread rapidly throughout the rest of the European continent. The killer arrived in the British Isles in 1348 and struck with such devastating force that it wiped out more than one third of the population. Infected oriental fleas, hosted by black rats, are believed to have caused the outbreak of the insidious disease.

Norman Ireland was ravaged in 1348 when the Bubonic plague reached the island. Better known as the 'Black death,' the plague devastated the well populated Norman towns, villages and hamlets. Studies show that the population was so decimated, oak, birch and ash forests enjoyed a rapid rise in growth during the late fourteenth century, testimony to the reduction in population. John Clyn, a noted scholar monk from Kilkenny, whose written record is considered to be the only eye witness account, stated, "the plague first appeared in Howth or Dalkey and spread to Dublin and Drogheda by late July or early August 1348." Clyn further states, "from very fear and horror, men were seldom brave enough to perform the works of piety and mercy, such as visiting the sick and burying the dead." The plague continued to ravage Dublin and Drogheda from August to December and set the scene for what would follow nationwide.

Many people resorted to religion, going on pilgrimages and praying. All public functions were cancelled and there is a pause in the record of both parliamentary and court sessions between 1348 and 1350. Clyn writes, "by this stage, the pestilence was highly contagious, such that whosoever touched the sick or the dead was immediately infected and died." Clyn also emphasizes the devastation when he wrote, "there was hardly a house in which one only had died, but as a rule man and wife with their children and all the family went the common way of death." Monasteries were particularly hard-hit and many Franciscan friars died in Drogheda, with many more dying in Dublin. A scribe in the Franciscan friary at Nenagh, County Tipperary tells us that "this unheard of mortality spread to surrounding towns and villages, many of which were left without inhabitants."

The native Irish populace, because they lived a more rural and widely dispersed existence, for the most part, survived in greater numbers. In the wake of the Black Death, the Irish language and customs enjoyed a resurgence and the English controlled area of the country was reduced to a small, heavily fortified area on the east coast, known as the Pale. The native language and customs came to dominate the country once again as the English-controlled areas shrank. When the 'Black Death' retreated, it left in its wake a decimated and devastated world with more than 100 million people dead. One of the results was a marked decrease in the number of laborers available for work. This loss of manpower led to a shortage of farm labor, and a corresponding rise in wages. The great landowners struggled with the shortage of manpower and the resulting inflation in the cost of labor.

To curb the rise in wages, King Edward III and his parliament responded with the Ordinance of Laborers in 1349, followed by the Statute of Laborers in 1351. Because so many people gathered at a fair, it quickly turned into the major place for matching workers and employers. Hiring fairs continued well into the twentieth century, up to the Second World War in some places, but their function as employment exchanges was diminished by the Corn Production Act 1917. This legislation guaranteed minimum prices for wheat and oats, specified a minimum wage for agricultural workers and established the Agricultural Wages Board, to ensure stability for farmers and a share of this stability for agricultural workers. Hiring fairs were common in England and Scotland for many years before they came to Ireland. Since both employers and laborers had an interest in what was said at these sessions, they were common ground on which to meet, and naturally enough some made their agreements there and then.

7 Lionel of Antwerp

Lionel of Antwerp, known as the Duke of Clarence, was the third son of Edward III. When he was a child he was married to Elizabeth de Burgh, daughter of William de Burgh, 3rd Earl of Ulster. At 14 years old he took over his wife Elisabeth's property and other holdings in Ireland. He became Edward III's representative in England and in 1355 he was made the Earl of Ulster. Afraid that Norman control was slipping from his grasp, King Edward sent his son Lionel to Ireland in an attempt to regain control. In 1361, Lionel, in command of a large army, landed in Dublin and immediately set out to recruit local Normans to bolster his army. After a series of failed attempts to overthrow the Irish in Leinster and Munster, Lionel retreated to Kilkenny, where, in 1366 he set up the 'Parliament of Kilkenny' and convened a conference.

The aim of the conference was to pass legislation that would hopefully staunch the decline of Norman control. New laws were enacted in which Normans were barred from inter-marrying with native Irish, speaking the Irish language, playing the game of hurling, using Irish law or dress, and listening to Irish music or stories. Thankfully, few obeyed the new laws as many Norman families, by that time in Ireland for two hundred years, considered themselves completely Irish and no longer felt patriotic to the English crown. Lionel died in 1367, with his futile attempt to regain control a complete disaster and ensured that his name was relegated to the realm of failure.

8   Richard II

Richard II, also known as Richard of Bordeaux, was King of England from 1377 until he was deposed in 1399. Richard, the son of Edward, known as the *Black Prince*, was born in Bordeaux during the reign of his grandfather, Edward III. In 1377, at age ten, Richard became the newly crowned monarch of England. Like his predecessor, he too felt that he could impose his will in Ireland using brute force. In 1394 he landed at Waterford with a large force of 10,000 men and the new invention, artillery. Faced with such overwhelming odds, many of the Irish nobility surrendered to Richard. Anyone who submitted and swore allegiance were allowed to keep their lands and titles, with the exception of the Irish Rulers of Leinster. Richard had them evicted and planned to plant English Lords on their lands. In the interim, the land was temporarily left unoccupied, and when Richard departed Ireland in 1399, full-scale war erupted. After the assassination of Richard's viceroy, the Lords of Leinster returned to their lands and once again regained control. Not long afterwards, his cousin Henry, who would later ascend the throne as Henry IV, murdered Richard.

Chapter 7
Upheaval and Treachery

1   The ascension of the Earls

In 1337 England and France went to war, known as the 'hundred years' war, a war which lasted until 1453. This conflict drained badly needed manpower from Ireland and further weakened the Norman hold. The Norman decline continued for the next fifty years and by 1450, English control in Ireland had been reduced to a twenty mile-wide strip of land around Dublin, known as the *Pale*. The Normans fiercely defended this area, and the Irish were unable to completely drive them out. The *Pale*, from the Latin word *Palus* meaning 'stake' or 'fence,' had been reduced in size by the late fifteenth century to an area along the east coast that stretched from Dalkey just south of Dublin all the way north to the town of Dundalk. Inland, the boundary went from Naas and Leixlip in the Earldom of Kildare and north towards Trim and Kells in County Meath, and until today, many townlands in this district, still have English and French names. The *Pale* was surrounded with a sturdy fence, ditch and earthen rampart, constructed in an effort to keep the Irish out, (beyond the *Pale*) parts of which can still be seen on the grounds of what is now Clongowes Wood College. The remaining English Lords whose estates were sited within the *Pale* continued to exist, formed alliances with the neighboring Irish and became extremely powerful.

Outside the *Pale*, particularly in the province of Munster, former Norman Lords now considered themselves to be completely Irish, and many of them joined with the native Irish in their opposition to the English.At that time two of the most powerful Irish families in Ireland were the Butlers and the FitzGeralds. Both families were descended from Norman settlers, but had lived in Ireland for so long that they regarded themselves as purely Irish. The FitzGeralds, descendants of Gerald of Windsor, were also known as the Geraldines and hated the English more than any other family in Ireland. The Butlers swore fealty and gave their support to the English king and for this reason, the two families were often at loggerheads and regularly went to war with each other. In 1463, one of the FitzGerald earls made an unprecedented move and sided with the English. He was kidnapped and murdered by members of his own family in 1468 and set the scene for the next invasion of Ireland.

2   A Temporary Peace

In 1492, the same year that Christopher Columbus purportedly discovered the New World, an incident, with far reaching effects, took place in a chapter house attached to Saint Patrick's Cathedral in Dublin. The incident ended a long running and bloody feud between two of Ireland's most powerful dynasties, the FitzGeralds and the Butlers. The FitzGeralds, staunch supporters of the fight to remove the English from Ireland, often went to war with the Butlers who swore their allegiance to the English crown.

In 1485, with help from the Butler family, Henry 7th ascended the throne of England as the first monarch of the House of Tudor. His coronation was opposed by many of the Irish Earls, particularly Gerald Mor Fitzgerald, the 8th Earl of Kildare. In 1492, a long running dispute between the two foremost families in medieval Ireland, the Butlers, (Earls of Ormond) and the FitzGeralds, (Earls of Kildare) was resolved by a brave act and an equally brave response.

James Butler (Black James,) the nephew of the Earl of Ormond, while on the run from FitzGerald's soldiers, took sanctuary in the Chapter House of St. Patrick's Cathedral in Dublin. Although he was in a superior position and with his army surrounding 'Black James' and his men, FitzGerald decided to put an end to the bloody feud. He pleaded with 'Black James' through the Chapter House's oak door, to come out, meet with him and discuss a peace treaty. Fearing a trap, James refused and prepared to do battle. After numerous failed attempts, FitzGerald ordered his soldiers to cut a hole in the middle of the door. Then, after explaining that he truly wished to bring peace between the families, FitzGerald put his arm through the hole and offered his hand to James. It was a risky move as one of James's heavily armed men could easily have hacked FitzGeralds arm off. Despite the fear and mistrust, James shook hands with FitzGerald and ended the dispute.

Though the Chapter House has long been demolished, it was originally located in the South Transept of St Patrick's Cathedral. The door of the Chapter House is on display in the cathedral's north transept where it is now known as the *Door of Reconciliation*. This event is locally credited as an etymology of the term to 'chance one's arm,' which means "to perform an action in the face of probable failure."

3   Conquest by Henry VII

In 1485, with help from the Butler's, the Earls of Tipperary, Henry 7th ascended the throne of England as the first monarch of the House of Tudor. His coronation was opposed by many of the Irish Earls, including Gerald Mor Fitzgerald, the 8th Earl of Kildare, this despite the fact that one of his relatives had supported the previous king. A major problem for Henry was the fact that his predecessor had allowed Gerald Mor to gain so much power that he was now becoming a threat to the English control of the Pale. After careful study, Henry came to the conclusion that English power in Ireland was tenuous and plotted to restore full control.

4   Gerald FitzGerald

Gerald FitzGerald, was the son of Thomas FitzGerald, 7th Earl of Kildare and Jane FitzGerald, the daughter of the usurper James FitzGerald, 6th Earl of Desmond. He was made Lord Deputy in 1477, and in 1478 inherited the title Earl of Kildare. FitzGerald managed to hold on to his title even after the English House of York was toppled and Henry VII became king. Fitzgerald blatantly disobeyed King Henry on many occasions and fully supported the pretender to the throne of England and the Lordship of Ireland, Lambert Simnel. Henry was wise enough to realize that he needed Fitzgerald to rule in Ireland, but also knew that he would be difficult to control. Simnel's attempt to seize the throne ended in disaster at the Battle of Stoke and many of his supporters, were killed. Henry, now assured of his kingship, could afford to be magnanimous and pardoned both Simnel and FitzGerald. FitzGerald was clever enough not to commit himself to the cause of the next pretender Perkin Warbeck, despite Henry's taunt that "the Irish nobility would crown an ape to secure power for themselves."

The situation worsened in 1487, when Henry's opponent to the throne, Edward, arrived in Dublin and gained the allegiance of the FitzGeralds, who then crowned him as the true King of England. Henry was furious and had Gerald Mor kidnapped and sent to the dreaded Tower of London. Henry then passed a law removing the independence of the Irish parliament within the confines of the *Pale*, and ordered that, in the future, Ireland was to be ruled directly from London. Up to this time, Fitzgerald had been enjoying a period of relative peace and independence from English rule. While incarcerated, Fitzgerald was dealt another harsh blow when news reached him of his wife's death. At his trial in 1496, he was accused of being a traitor but managed to convince King Henry that the ruling factions in Ireland were 'false knaves.' Surprisingly, Henry appointed him as Lord Deputy of Ireland, saying, "all Ireland cannot govern this Earl; then let this Earl govern all Ireland" and allowed him to marry Elizabeth St. John, a distant cousin of the King, after which Fitzgerald returned to Ireland in triumph and once there, ruled with an iron fist.

5   FitzGerald's Treachery

FitzGerald, now considered "more Irish than the Irish themselves," mounted a series of cruel and violent military campaigns against his fellow Irishmen. He suppressed a rebellion in the city of Cork in 1500 after he had the city's mayor hanged. He raised an army against the rebels in Connacht in 1504, and defeated them at the Battle of Knockdoe. In 1512, he invaded O'Neill of Clandeboye's territory, captured him and took the O'Neills' castle in Belfast. Then, for reasons unknown, FitzGerald marched further north and ravaged the Bissett family's lordship in the Glens of Antrim. A year later, on an expedition against the O'Carrolls, he was mortally wounded while watering his horse in Kilkea. He was brought back to Kildare, where he died in September 1513.

6   Henry the VIII

Henry VIII, from the House of Tudor, was crowned King of England in 1509 on the death of his father Henry VII. He was the first English born King of Ireland, and also claimed sovereignty over the Kingdom of France. Henry VIII was the second monarch of the Tudor dynasty and is primarily known for his role in the separation from the Catholic Church of Rome. Married six times, Henry was eventually excommunicated after he defied the Popes ruling against divorce and his marriage to Anne Boleyn. His arguments with the Papacy in Rome led to the separation from the Catholic church and the setting up of the Church of England with Henry as it's supreme leader. From then on the Henry's form of religion was to be the only one in all lands controlled by him which included Catholic Ireland.

In 1513, Gerald Mor Fitzgerald was succeeded by his son Gerald Og Fitzgerald who continued to rule the *Pale* in the name of the new monarch, King Henry VIII. Gerald Og's power started to wane after Henry married Anne Boleyn, who was from the rival Butler family, the FitzGerald's mortal enemies. His friendship with Henry began to diminish at this time also. In 1533 Gerald Og was ordered to a meeting with Henry in London. Meanwhile, in Ireland, a false rumor was deliberately spread that Henry had Gerald Og executed. Gerald Og's son then issued a statement that the FitzGeralds would 'no longer act as the King's deputy in Ireland.' This was seen as a direct defiance of the King's rule and considered to be a mutinous act. Henry acted immediately; he ordered the roundup of all FitzGeralds, had them murdered, their lands confiscated and their castles razed. The area known as the *Pale* was extended and now included the FitzGerald's former kingdom of Kildare. In an effort to stem the rebellion started by the murder of the FitzGeralds, and with only a few Irish Earls still loyal to him, Henry entered negotiations and signed deals with the remaining Earls, promising them land and titles. From this point forward, the *Pale* was ruled solely by the English and not by Irish Earls. By employing these clever tactics, Henry managed to regain control of most of Ireland in a very short period of time, with relatively little bloodshed.

> Between 1536 and 1541 Henry VIII enacted a policy that became known as the 'Suppression of the Monasteries.' All Catholic monasteries, priories, convents and friaries in England, Wales and Ireland were shut down, their income, assets, and lands confiscated. Anyone who opposed this barbaric act were put to the sword without mercy. The closure of the monasteries was one of the most destructive events to occur in English history. In Ireland this was viewed as a direct assault on the Catholic religion and way of life but sadly, was only a foretaste of what was to come in the near future. Eventually, Henry, by then extremely overweight, coupled with his declining health, died a horrible death at the age of 55, in January 1547 at the Palace of Whitehall. His alleged last words: "Monks! Monks! Monks!" were probably a reference to the monks he had tortured, executed and expelled during the 'Suppression of the Monasteries.' After his death, his only legitimate son, Edward, inherited the Crown, becoming Edward VI.

Interestingly, in 1539, the property of one of the monasteries that had been seized, St. Andrew's Priory, was sold off to Lawrence Washington, ancestor of the first United States President, George Washington.

7   Edward VI

There were three distinct forms of religious worship during the time of Henry VIII and Edward VI's reigns: Catholicism, which owed its allegiance to the Church of Rome with the Pope as supreme leader. Protestantism claimed its allegiance to Martin Luther, its founder, and Presbyterianism owed its allegiance to John Galvin and the Scottish reformer John Knox.

In 1547 Henry VIII's only legitimate son Edward, was crowned King of England and Ireland. He has the distinction of being the third king of the Tudor dynasty and the first monarch raised under the mantle of the budding Protestant religion. Since Edward was then only nine years old, he was not able to rule in his own right, but in his will, Henry stipulated that, until Edward reached the age of eighteen, a Regency Council, with handpicked members, should act as advisors to him and ensure adherence to Henry's policies. Edward's reign was dogged by widespread economic problems and social unrest that erupted into full scale street riots and rebellion in 1549. Wars with Scotland and France were not going according to plan and forced Edward to retreat and start peace negotiations. His continued transformation of the Catholic Church into the new religion now included the outlawing of the Catholic Mass, the abolition of celibacy among clerics, the removal of Latin and the imposition of the English language in all church services. These fundamental changes had a profound effect in Ireland.

Also in 1549, the Church of England was altered again by Edward. Winds of change were blowing in many European countries with large numbers of Roman Catholics, led by a German minister named Martin Luther, protesting against the continual corruption in the Roman Catholic church at the time. Their protests and actions became known as the 'Protestant Reformation,' and their followers were called 'Protestants.' Edward became interested in the Protestant movement as he felt that the Church of England was still too Roman Catholic. He decreed that confession, processions and the belief that bread and wine changed form during Mass, be removed. In this way, the Church of England became much more similar to the new Protestant churches that were appearing all over Europe. Most Irish refused to accept these changes to the church, not least because the new rules were written in English whereas they could only speak Irish. Therefore, Ireland remained Roman Catholic while England gradually became more and more Protestant.

At age 15, Edward fell ill and when his sickness was discovered to be terminal, he and his Council drew up a 'Devise for the Succession,' in an attempt to prevent the country's return to Catholicism. Edward named his first cousin, Lady Jane Grey, as his heir and excluded his half-sisters, Mary and Elizabeth. However, this decision was disputed following Edward's death, and Jane was deposed by Mary within 13 days. As queen, Mary set out to reverse her predecessor Edward's Protestant reforms.

8   Mary I (Bloody Mary)

Mary I was the Queen of England and Ireland from July 1553 until her death. She was the only child of Henry VIII and his first wife Catherine of Aragon, to survive into adulthood. Her younger half-brother Edward VI (son of Henry and Jane Seymour) had succeeded their father in 1547. When Edward became mortally ill in 1553, he attempted to remove Mary from the line of succession because of religious differences. On his death their first cousin once removed, Lady Jane Grey, was proclaimed queen. Mary assembled an army and deposed Jane, who was ultimately beheaded. Mary was the first queen regnant of England and in 1554, she married Philip of Spain, becoming queen consort of Habsburg, Spain on Phillip's accession in 1556. As the fourth crowned monarch of the Tudor dynasty, Mary I is remembered for her restoration of Roman Catholicism. During her five-year reign, she had hundreds of religious dissenters burned at the stake in a series of persecutions. Hundreds more were forced into exile. Her widespread executions of Protestants led to her nickname "Bloody Mary." After her death in 1558, the re-establishment of Roman Catholicism was reversed by her half-sister and successor Elizabeth I, daughter of Henry VIII and Anne Boleyn.

9   Elizabeth I

Elizabeth I was the Queen of England and Ireland from 1558 until her death. Sometimes called the 'Virgin Queen,' Elizabeth was the fifth and last monarch of the Tudor dynasty. She was the daughter of Henry VIII and Anne Boleyn, who had been executed two and a half years after Elizabeth's birth. Anne's marriage to Henry VIII was annulled, and Elizabeth was declared to be illegitimate. Her half-brother, Edward VI, ruled until his death in 1553, bequeathing the crown to Lady Jane Grey and ignoring the claims of his two half-sisters, Elizabeth and the Roman Catholic Mary. Edward's wishes were not accepted and Mary became queen after deposing

Lady Jane Grey. During Mary's reign, Elizabeth was imprisoned for nearly a year because of her support for the Protestant rebels.

After her ascension, Elizabeth set out to fully restore the Protestant religion and eventually made England Protestant once more. Next, despite the huge expenses incurred by her efforts to colonize the new world, (America) she set her sights on Ireland, a much more convenient place to colonize, it being closer to home. From the outset, her reign was dogged by continuous rebellions. An attack by the O'Neills of Tyrone was defeated in 1561 and two revolts by the FitzGeralds of Cork and Kerry were put down in 1575 and 1580. Elizabeth took advantage of the defeat of the FitzGeralds in Cork and initiated the plantation of Munster. After promises of land and wealth, many English families came and settled on what had formerly been FitzGerald property. The land was quickly farmed, towns built and by 1587, it was a thriving colony. The colony was devastated in 1598 by a series of well executed lightening attacks by the Irish forces in Munster, from which it never fully recovered, even so, many English families continued to live there, mostly in isolated areas.

Chapter 8
Rebels and Uprisings

1   The O'Neills

During the Middle Ages, the O'Neills of Tyrone were a well respected and powerful dynasty. Active politically and militarily throughout Ireland, they often sent troops to fight in campaigns within Ireland and also in Europe. From 1312 to 1318, the O'Neill kings were loyal supporters of King Robert Bruce and his brother Edward Bruce in their struggle for Scottish independence. They sent men and provisions in support of Edward in his attempt to become King of Ireland in 1315. Held in such high regard, in 1394 Richard II of England was prompted to refer to King Niall Mor as the "Le Grand O'Neill" during a friendly meeting of the two kings. In the fourteenth century Edward III of England called the Earl of Tyrone "the Great O'Neill" and invited him to join his campaign against the Scots, another O'Neill prince went with the English king on a crusade to the Holy Land. In 1493, Henry VII of England referred to Henry O'Neill, King of Tyrone, as "the Chief of the Irish Kings." The O'Neills' power and prestige in Ulster began to subside with the ascent of King Henry VIII in England in 1509. Soon after he took the English throne, Henry decided to take control of Ireland using a 'Papal Bull' which claimed to grant the control of Ireland to English kings. This was eventually rebuked by a rebellion in 1547 led by 'Silken' Thomas Fitzgerald. The O'Neills lent their support to their cousins the FitzGeralds, but when the rebellion failed, they had to use their considerable skills as politicians in an effort to keep the English from removing their power in Ulster.

Conn Bacach O'Neill

Henry VIII was concerned about the power the Irish kings wielded and devised to end the centuries old practice of each clan choosing and crowning their own kings, using the Brehon law system.

To achieve this, Henry put in place a more English system in which all would be subject to one ruler. He enacted and willfully enforced a new policy called 'Surrender and Regrant' whereby Irish monarchs were forced to surrender their titles and lands to the crown, and in return Henry appointed them as Earls of the Kingdom of Ireland and granted back to them their own lands. The last King of Tyrone and first Earldom was granted by Henry in 1542 to Conn Bacach O'Neill. The subservience of Conn O'Neill led to a 50-year civil war within Ulster that eventually caused the end of O'Neill power in 1607.

Shane O'Neill

Shane O'Neill (Shane the Proud,) was an Irish King of the O'Neill dynasty of Ulster in the mid sixteenth century. His career was marked by his ambition to attain overall sovereignty of the powerful O'Néill Mór clan of Tyrone. Achieving this would make him the head *rí ruirech*, the chief king, of the entire province. This brought him into direct conflict with other branches of the O'Neill clans and also caused problems with the English government. Shane's support was considered important by the English even during the time of his father Conn O'Neill, 1st Earl of Tyrone, but, after refusing requests from Thomas Radclyffe, the lord deputy of Ireland, Shane declined to support the English against the Scottish settlers on the coast of Antrim, and sided with the MacDonnell clans instead.

Turlough Luineach O'Neill (The O'Neill)

In 1569, Turlough Luineach O'Neill (The O'Neill) married Lady Agnes Campbell, daughter of Colin Campbell, 3rd Earl of Argyll, Scotland. Her dowry consisted of at least 1,200 gallowglass mercenaries, each with two squires as assistants. This made for a considerable fighting force and alliances made with the O'Donnell, MacDonnell and MacQuillan clans, ensured that Turlough was a force to be reckoned with. In approximately 1574 an expedition under Walter Devereux, the Earl of Essex, was sent against him, but had little success and in 1575 a treaty was arranged whereby Turlough received extensive grants of lands and permission to employ Gallowglasses and Scottish mercenaries. Another treaty in 1578, negotiated by Lady Agnes, Turlough's wife, consolidated his land holdings in Ulster, granted him a Knighthood and the British titles of Earl of Clanconnell and Baron of Clogher, for life.

On the outbreak of a rebellion in the province of Munster, Turlough entered secret talks with Spain and Scotland and for the next several years he continued to plot against the English authorities. Despite all of this intrigue, he kept control of Ulster until 1593, when he was forced by poor health and military setbacks to concede power to his main rival, Hugh O'Neill. Hugh O'Neill was the brother of Brian O'Neil whom Turlough had assassinated in 1562 during Shane O'Neill's absence at the court of Elizabeth I. Hugh, in 1595, seized the last castle still held by Turlough, razed it, and drove Turlough into hiding. Turlough died later that year and was buried at Ardstraw, the Franciscan Friary founded by his ancestors.

2   Ireland and the Spanish Armada

On a cold, stark night in August 1588, as a fierce gale subsided and the clouds slowly parted, light from a full autumn moon revealed a horrific scene strewn along the shoreline of Streedagh Strand in County Sligo, Ireland. The drowned corpses of 800 doomed sailors, washed up by the raging Atlantic Ocean waves, lay scattered among the rocks and sand; the bodies, already stripped of all items of value, were left as carrion for packs of starving wild dogs and flocks of hungry ravens. Broken chests full of gold, silver and jewels, were looted and carried off by bands of scavenging, local inhabitants. Concealed among the rushes, a short distance from the shore, a lone survivor, woken by the sounds of the feeding frenzy, wondered if he was having a horrible dream. Struggling upright, he propped himself on one elbow and let his gaze slowly wander the length of the strand, revealing the scene of utter carnage. As his terrified mind raced and tried to make sense of the awful sight before him, memories started to return and images of earlier events began to unfold. He remembered three ships fleeing in panic, a dangerously rocky shoreline, terrified fellow sailors, a violent storm and then... darkness.

Thirty years earlier In February 1558, Catholic Queen Mary I, Henry VIII's daughter, died and her half-sister Elizabeth ascended the throne of England. As Protestant Queen Elizabeth I, she set out to undo the religious reforms enacted by Mary and her husband and co-monarch, Philip II of Spain, also a devout Catholic. Even after his wife's death, Philip had no wish to sever his ties with England, and for many years maintained peace with England, and even defended Elizabeth from the Pope's threats of excommunication. He had also sent a proposal of marriage to Elizabeth, hoping that as her husband, he would be able to influence policy and further Catholic emancipation. Elizabeth delayed replying to Philip's proposal and in the interim, learned that Philip was also forging an alliance with France.

When she discovered that Philip signed the Treaty of Joinville with the Catholic League of France, Elizabeth formed an alliance between England and the Protestant rebels in the Netherlands. She also enacted a policy of piracy against Spanish trade and began to plunder the great Spanish treasure ships returning from the New world. When the Treaty of Nonsuch was signed at Nonsuch Palace in Surrey by Elizabeth in 1585, and which promised troops and supplies to the Dutch rebels, sworn enemies of Spain, Philip considered this an act of war and initiated plans for an invasion of England. The last straw for Philip was the execution of Mary, Queen of Scots, in 1587, which ended Philip's hopes of placing a Catholic on the English throne. He turned instead to more direct plans to invade England and return the country to Catholicism.

At the end of May 1588, with the blessing of Pope Sixtus V, a fleet of 130 ships set sail from A Coruna, Spain under the command of the Duke of Medina Sidonia, a high-born courtier. Medina Sidonia, although a competent soldier and distinguished administrator, had no naval experience and wrote to Philip expressing grave doubts about the planned campaign, but his letter was prevented from reaching the King on the grounds that God would ensure them success. The fleet, known as the Spanish Armada, was composed of 130 ships, 8,000 sailors, 18,000 soldiers, and was armed with 1,500 brass and 1,000 iron guns. From the Spanish Netherlands, a further 30,000 soldiers, under the command of the Duke of Parma, waited for the arrival of the Armada. The plan was to use the cover of the warships to convey the army on barges to a place near London, and then march on the city.

All told, 55,000 men were to have been mustered an imposing army for that time. On the day the Armada set sail, Elizabeth's ambassador in the Netherlands, Valentine Dale, met Parma's representatives in peace talks, but in July the negotiations were abandoned, and the English fleet stood at anchor in Plymouth, awaiting news of Spanish movements. Philip initially planned for an attack on three fronts, starting with a raid on Scotland, while the main Armada would attack the Isle of Wight, then establish a safe anchorage in the Solent. The Duke of Parma would follow with a large army from the Low Countries and sail across the English Channel. The Duke was uneasy about mounting such an invasion without the possibility of surprise, was wary of the costs that such a venture would incur, and advised Philip to abandon or at least postpone the overly ambitious plan.

The revised plan entailed sailing north into the English Channel, establish a safe anchorage and then rendezvous with Parma's army at Dunkirk, France. Unfortunately, for Philip, his plan had little chance of success from the outset, mainly because of lengthy delays, poor lines of communication, the lack of a deep bay for anchorage and violent storms. As the battle commenced a storm struck the English Channel, which devastated large numbers of the Spanish fleet. There was one hard fought battle against the English navy, but the Spanish were forced into a retreat, and the majority of their ships were destroyed by the harsh weather.

The Armada chose not to attack the English fleet at Plymouth, and failed to establish a temporary anchorage in the Solent after one Spanish ship had been captured by Francis Drake in the English Channel.

The fleet finally dropped anchor off Calais, and while waiting communications from the Duke of Parma's army, was routed by an English fire ship attack. In the Battle of Gravelines the Spanish fleet was further damaged and forced to abandon its rendezvous with Parma's army. Despite all of the setbacks, they managed to regroup and, driven by southwest winds, sailed north, with the English fleet following them up the east coast of England. In their haste to flee the relentless English pursuit, many of the Spanish ship captains ordered the anchor chains cut, an act that would prove to be disastrous later on as events unfolded.

Following its defeat at the battle of Gravelines the Armada had attempted to return home through the North Atlantic. Unfortunately, a series of violent storms blew them off course and toward the west coast of Ireland, where, with no anchors to stabilize many of the ships, the Spanish Armada was doomed. When word of the Armadas' fate reached Dublin, Queen Elizabeth issued instructions to her government ministers, stating that any and all survivors found on Irish soil were to be immediately executed and anyone found rendering aid or shelter were to be given the same punishment. Soldiers on horseback were dispatched to patrol the coastline and search for survivors. As many as 24 ships were wrecked on the rocky coastline from Antrim in the north to Kerry in the south, and it is estimated that up to 5000 sailors and soldiers died in Ireland. Those who managed to escape the dragnet fled Ireland, with many crossing over into Scotland. It was reported that, when Philip learned of the result of the expedition, he declared, "I sent the Armada against men, not God's winds and waves."

On Streedagh Strand, the survivor Francisco de Cuéllar, a Spanish sea captain, drifted in and out of consciousness until the sound of horse hoofs pounding along the shoreline jolted him back to reality. Shaking his head and rubbing his eyes, still unsure if he was dead or alive, awake or an unwilling participant in some hellish nightmare, he got to his knees and peered through the rushes. In the distance, close to the waters' edge, he could see the horsemen, at full gallop, approach his place of concealment.

His heart sank as he realized that the riders were English soldiers and knew discovery would mean instant death. Frantic, he looked closer at his surroundings and noticed a low stone wall about fifty yards from where he knelt. Mustering his strength, and not daring to stand upright, he crawled on his hands and knees until he reached the wall; then with a quick glance behind, scrambled over the top and lay silent and exhausted on the other side.

With no time to linger, he left the shelter of the wall and moved cautiously until he entered a large wooded area where he would be out of sight of the soldiers on the strand. Upright, he ran for what seemed an eternity, tree branches whipping and stinging his face and arms and briars impeding his progress. As the morning sun began to rise and warm him, strangely, he felt safe in the woods, and was reminded of his father and the happy times they spent together exploring the forest close to his hometown of Cuellar in the Spanish province of Segovia. He had spent long hours there in wide eyed wonderment and recalled his father teaching him the names of every tree and every bird. A memory flashed through his mind reminding of something his father had told him all those years ago. He had once asked him what would happen if they ever got lost in the woods. His father had replied that it was impossible to get lost and told him that as moss only grows on the north side of tree trunks, it would always be easy to find your bearings. He would use that advice as his guide and hoped that he could outrun his pursuers and continue to head north.

Out of breath he slowed to a walking pace, occasionally glancing fearfully over his shoulder and as he came to the woods edge, met an elderly woman who was driving cattle into hiding. She told him that English soldiers were searching for survivors and had already killed 100 captives who had sought refuge in her village. Before parting, she warned him to stay out of the road and to travel only at night. Leaving the shelter and relative safety of the woods, his first foray onto open ground did not go well for him. With the woods behind him he walked until he came across a small stone building set on a slight rise close to a narrow stream. Hoping for shelter and maybe some food, he approached the building warily and as he got nearer he could see that it was a church which had been sacked and set on fire, smoke still rising from the charred roof timbers. Rounding the corner, he was shocked to see the bodies of twelve sailors hanging from nooses tied to the iron bars on the windows. Terrified and desperate, he turned and ran blindly back to the shelter and safety provided him by the trees. What followed was a seven-month long fight for survival by de Cuellar. Freezing, alone and scared he lived on a diet of wild berries and watercress and came close to death several times. Fortunately for him, during his travels along the west coast of Ireland, he was befriended and given food and shelter by two powerful Irish chieftains, O'Rourke and MacClancy. The chieftains, themselves no stranger to English wrath and violence, helped de Cuellar to travel to Donegal in the north of the country, where he eventually boarded a ship bound for Scotland. A full and detailed account of his adventures survives and can be read in a letter written by him soon after his escape from Ireland. The chieftain O'Rourke was hanged at London for treason in 1590; the charges against him included giving aid to survivors of the Armada. MacClancy was captured by the English in 1590 and beheaded.

After the Armada disaster, de Cuéllar served in the army of Philip II under Alexander Farnese, Duke of Parma, Count Fuentes and Count Mansfeld. Between 1589 and 1598 he served variously in the Siege of París, the Campaigns of de Laón, Corbel, Capela, Châtelet, Dourlens, Cambrai, Calais, and Ardres, and in the siege of Hults. In 1599 and 1600 he served under Charles Emmanuel I, Duke of Savoy in the war of Piamonte. In 1600, he was in Naples with Viceroy Lemos. In 1601, he was commissioned to return to America and served as infantry captain in a galleon to Islas de Barlovento (Windward Islands), but didn't sail in don Luis Fernández de Córdova's navy until 1602. It was his last military service. He lived in Madrid in the period 1603–1606, hoping for new commissions in America.

Chapter 9
War and Intrigue

1   Rebellion

By 1598, Ulster was the last province to remain purely Celtic with the rest of the country now a conglomerate of many different cultural influences. Ulster held on to its identity mainly because it was defended by a number of strong, determined clans and geographically, it was far enough away from the seat of English power which was confined mostly to the south east coast and points further south. Hugh O'Neill, the new Earl of *Tir Eoghain* (Tyrone) knew that the English control of the rest of Ireland was a threat to his Celtic heritage, Brehon laws and Catholic faith. Worried about the increasing strength of the English, he decided to attack first and organized his forces in preparation. The English, completely unprepared, found it difficult to repel Hugh's advances and after a series of violent offensives, were driven from the province. The English, deciding to cut their losses, dug-in around the borders of Ulster and built a series of well defended forts.

The new tactics now being used by the English forced Hugh O'Neill to attack their heavily defended forts, which gave the English the advantage; but despite these new tactics, it wasn't until 1601 at the battle of Kinsale that O'Neill's troops were finally defeated. O'Neill and his armies retreated back to *Tir Eoghain* but refused to surrender. Rather than invading Ulster to rout O'Neill, the English strengthened their forts and started launching hit and run raids into Ulster, destroying crops, slaughtering livestock, burning storehouses and harassing O'Neill's army. By adopting these methods, they hoped to starve O'Neill into submission or force him to launch disorganized attacks. O'Neill did attack again, but was defeated by Lord Mountjoy at the battle of Omagh in 1602. In 1603, the O'Neill's and the English signed the Treaty of Mellifont which allowed O'Neill to keep his lands if he gave up his title and conformed to the rule of English law.

2   The Treaty of Mellifont

Following the English victory in the Battle of Kinsale, the leaders fighting in Cork returned to Ulster to protect their lands. The Lord Deputy of Ireland, Charles Blount, 8th Baron Mountjoy, had succeeded where his predecessor, Robert Devereux, 2nd Earl of Essex, had failed. However, Mountjoy knew that as long as Hugh O'Neill was still alive, albeit in hiding, he still posed a considerable threat. Most of the clan leaders who had sided with Hugh had been forced to submit to the crown, with the exception of Rory O'Donnell, Brian Og O'Rourke, Cuchonnacht Maguire (brother of Hugh Maguire), and Donal Cam O'Sullivan Beare, who, despite all efforts to force their surrender, still remained loyal to O'Neill. Early in 1603, queen Elizabeth ordered Mountjoy, at the head of a large army, to concentrate his efforts in the northern counties of Ulster and the province of Leinster. She further ordered him to destroy the rebellious clans, their lands, houses, castles, crops and livestock. Mountjoy did just as commanded and a country wide famine followed in which untold numbers perished.

In his defense, Mountjoy and the English Council had long urged Queen Elizabeth to make peace. The war in Ireland was incurring huge costs and a major part of the budget was diverted to maintain the 20,000 strong army assigned to suppress the Irish rebels. Elizabeth also maintained a second army of 12,000 in her defense of the Dutch royal family, a war that became known as the 'Eighty Years War.' Finally, drained by the monumental costs of both wars, Elizabeth dropped her demands for unconditional surrender and authorized Mountjoy to enter negotiations with Hugh O'Neill.

The agents authorized by the Lord Deputy to conduct the peace talks were Sir William Godolphin and Sir Garrett Moore, an ancestor of the Marquesses of Drogheda. The discussions were held at Mellifont Abbey, near the village of Ballymascanlan, County Louth. In early March 1603, O'Neill traveled from his house on the shores of Lough Neagh and met with Elizabeth's agents at Mellifont. During the long series of heated conversations, word reached the Lord deputy that Elizabeth was seriously ill and not expected to live. When Elizabeth died in late March 1603, and fearing that the news would force the talks to be abandoned, her death was kept secret from the negotiators until the talks were concluded.

3   The terms of the Treaty

On the 31st of March, 1603, Hugh O'Neill submitted to the Crown of England. After his submission, he was pardoned. The pardon and terms were considered to be very generous at the time.

1   In return for renouncing the Gaelic title, Uí Néill, he would be known as the Earl of Tyrone.

2   He would be allowed to take a seat in the Irish House of Lords.

3   He would retain his territory except for Catholic church property.

4   He would swear an oath of loyalty to the Crown.

5   Brehon law would be replaced with English law.

6   He would no longer be permitted to support the Gaelic Bards.

7   English would be the official language.

8   Catholic Colleges and Churches could not be built on his property.

4   Flight of the Earls

Realizing his mistake too late, on September 14, 1607, Hugh O'Neill, Rory O'Donnell, Brian Og O'Rourke, Cuchonnacht Maguire, and Donal Cam O'Sullivan Beare, together with their many followers left Ireland for Spain. Their plan was to enlist new armies in France and Spain, return to Ireland and oust the English settlers who had taken their titles and lands. Unfortunately, O'Neill and O'Donnell both died in exile and the planned return to Ireland and subsequent rebellion, never took place. This singular event became known as the 'Flight of the Earls' and signaled the death knell for the age old Gaelic traditions in Ulster.

5   Aftermath of the Treaty

Even with Hugh O'Neill and his followers gone, the English still felt threatened and believed that the Treaty of Mellifont was not enough to keep control of Ulster. They knew that the Irish Earls had many friends and supporters in Ireland as well as in France and Spain, and feared that Spain would at some future date, supply the Ulstermen with arms to launch another uprising against them. In an effort to stabilize their position and hammer home the advantage, they decided to plant Ulster with Protestant settlers. So this time, having learned valuable lessons from past failed plantations, particularly in Munster, the new settlers would be planted in Ulster. In 1609 the English mapped out 4,000,000 acres of land and started distribution in 1610. Counties Down, Monaghan and Antrim were planted privately. Counties Derry and Armagh were planted with English families and Tyrone and Donegal were planted with Scots. Counties Fermanagh and Cavan were planted with a mixture of both Scots and English. The new settlers were to live in specially built, heavily fortified settlements, that were known as 'Plantation Towns.' With these settlers came a new set of religious beliefs, called Presbyterianism. Totally different from Catholicism and Protestantism, the new form followed a more puritan style of worship and soon came to dominate. In this way Ulster became culturally very different from the rest of the British Isles. Sporadic attacks by native Ulstermen were dealt with ruthlessly and many offenders rounded up, imprisoned or deported. The Plantation of Ulster went on to become the most successful plantation of all.

6   James I of Ireland

James was the son of Mary, Queen of Scots, and a great-great-grandson of Henry VII, King of England and Lord of Ireland. He was born Catholic, but soon after his mother Mary was forced to abdicate the throne of Scotland, James was kidnapped by Protestant rebels and brought to Stirling castle where he was raised as a Protestant. He was crowned King of Scotland as James VI in 1567 and King of England and Ireland as James I in 1603. James, from the House of Stuart, took the Scottish throne at the age of thirteen months, after the death of the last Tudor monarch of England and Ireland, Elizabeth I, who died without having children. He reigned over all three kingdoms for twenty-two years, a period that became known as the Jacobean era.

Basing his seat of power in London, he returned only once to Scotland. During his reign, the Plantation of Ulster and the large scale colonization of the new world (America) began. James, was, among his many other accomplishments, a noted and prolific author, widely known for compiling two important books: The King James version of the bible and a guide book on the subject of witchcraft and how to identify witches, titled Daemonologie. The pilgrims would bring copies of these writings with them to the new world and use them with terrifying results, in Salem, Mass. James abhorred all things Catholic and from the beginning he set out to eradicate all traces of the 'heretical religion.' Persecutions of Catholics were commonplace and executions were carried out on a regular basis. There were several failed assassination plots hatched against James and his followers during his reign, culminating with the infamous Gunpowder Plot of 1605.

7   Early Plots

In 1603, troubled by the widespread persecutions and murders of Catholics, several members of the Catholic clergy decided to take matters into their own hands. In what became known as the 'Bye Plot,' two priests, William Watson and William Clark, planned to kidnap James and hold him in the Tower of London until he agreed to be more tolerant towards Catholics. News of the plot reached the Bishop George Blackwell, who instructed his priests to have no part in any such schemes. At about the same time, Sir George Brooke, Lord Cobham, Lord Grey de Wilton, Griffin Markham and Walter Raleigh hatched what became known as the 'Main Plot,' which intended to remove James and his family and install Catholic Arbella Stuart as Queen. They approached Henry IV of France for funding, but were turned down and all those involved in both plots were arrested in July and tried later in 1603. Sir George Brooke was executed, but at the eleventh hour, James reprieved Cobham, Grey, and Markham while they were on the scaffold. Raleigh, who had watched while his colleagues trembled in fear, and who was due to be executed a few days later, was also pardoned. The two priests, after condemnation by the Pope, were executed.

8   The Gunpowder Plot

"Remember, remember the fifth of November, the Gunpowder treason and plot.

I know of no reason why the Gunpowder treason should ever be forgot."

In 1605, a plan to assassinate King James I and his ministers was hatched by a group of English Catholics, led by a dissenter named Robert Catesby. The plot, an attempt to spark a revolt throughout England, Scotland and Ireland, was devised with the ultimate aim of installing James' nine-year-old daughter, Princess Elizabeth, as the Catholic Queen of England. The plan was to blow up the House of Lords during the state opening of England's Parliament on 5 November, 1605. When it became clear that the long awaited religious reforms and tolerance of Catholics was not going to happen under James' reign, Catesby set the plan in motion. He handpicked a group of like-minded individuals that included John Wright, Thomas Wintour, Thomas Percy, Robert Keyes, Thomas Bates, Robert

Wintour, Christopher Wright, John Grant, Ambrose Rookwood, Sir Everard Digby, Francis Tresham and Guido Fawkes. Fawkes, who had many years of military experience, was put in charge of the gunpowder.

Unfortunately for them, their plans were revealed in an anonymous letter which was delivered to William Parker, 4th Baron Monteagle on 26 October, 1605. During a search of the House of Lords at about midnight on 4 November, 1605, Fawkes was arrested when he was discovered guarding thirty-six barrels of gunpowder, enough explosives that if ignited, would undoubtedly raze the building. The plotters fled London when they learned of the plot's discovery but were eventually rounded up and sent to the ominous Tower of London to await trial. At the trial held on 27 January 1606, eight of the survivors, including Fawkes, were convicted and sentenced to be hung, drawn and quartered. As Fawkes stood awaiting his turn, he threw himself from the scaffold breaking his neck, thus saving himself the ignominity of the hangman's rope and subsequent dismemberment. Details of the plot were allegedly known by the principal Jesuit of England, Father Henry Garnet. Garnet was arrested, convicted of treason and sentenced to death, even though serious doubts were cast on how much he really knew. As the plot was revealed to him through the sacred act of confession, his argument being that he couldn't inform the authorities because of the confidentiality of confession.

The conspirators' principal aim was to kill King James, but many other important targets would also be present at the State Opening, including the monarch's nearest relatives and members of the Privy Council. The senior judges of the English legal system, most of the Protestant aristocracy, and the bishops of the Church of England would all have attended in their capacity as members of the House of Lords, along with the members of the House of Commons. Another important objective was the kidnapping of the King's daughter, third in the line of succession, Princess Elizabeth. Once James and his Parliament were dead, the plotters intended to install Elizabeth on the English throne as a titular Queen.

9   The Penal Laws

"all popish archbishops, bishops, vicars-general, deans, jesuits, monks, friars, and all other regular popish clergy shall depart out of this kingdom before the 1st day of May, 1698, and if any of said ecclesiastical persons shall after that day be in this kingdom, they shall suffer imprisonment, and remain in prison until transported out of his Majesty's dominions, wherever his Majesty or the chief governors of this kingdom shall see fit, and if any person so transported shall return, he shall be guilty of high treason."

Signed by James I

The failure of the Gunpowder Plot in 1605 had a disastrous effect in Ireland. In 1607 King James enacted a series of draconian and far reaching laws designed to eradicate Catholicism in one generation. The 'Penal Laws' as they became known, were a set of rules to be unwaveringly adhered to by all Catholics and dissenting Presbyterians. From 1607, Catholics were barred from holding public office or serving in the Irish Army. In 1613, the constituencies of the Irish House of Commons were altered to give plantation settlers a majority. In addition, Catholics in all three Kingdoms had to pay 'recusant fines' for non-attendance at Anglican services. Catholic churches were transferred to the Anglican Church of Ireland. Catholic services, however, were generally tacitly tolerated as long as they were conducted in private. Catholic priests were also tolerated, but bishops were forced to operate in secret.

Catholic resentment was a factor in starting the Irish Rebellion of 1641 and the establishment of Confederate Ireland from 1642 with Papal support, that was eventually put down in the Cromwellian conquest of Ireland in 1649–53. After the Act of Settlement in 1652, Catholics were barred from membership in the Irish Parliament, and the major landholders had most of their lands confiscated under the Adventurers Act. They were also banned from living in towns for a short period. Catholic clergy were expelled from the country and were liable to instant execution when found. Many recusants had to worship in secret at gathering places (such as Mass rocks) in the countryside and the mass rock became a symbol of Catholic rebellion against James and his intolerant policies.

10   The Mass Rock

It looked sad and forlorn sitting by the side of the Creamery road as though it knew that it had long been abandoned. I first noticed it one rainy afternoon when I was almost seven years old. I can still vividly recall the sweet scent of wild honeysuckle, hanging heavily on the air that day. At first glance, it was just another large, almost perfect, square shaped rock, covered with briars and moss, but there was an almost eerie attraction to it as if it wanted to tell me something. I didn't pay much attention that first time, as I was out rambling, but made a mental note to find out more about it and resolved to ask my father when I returned home.

Rambling is good for the soul as it brings us back to the time when we all were nomads, with no constraints, and in the soft, warm, misty Irish rain it is a wonderful, almost spiritual experience. There is a sense of freedom that's truly intoxicating. I went rambling most days after school and looked forward to the weekends. The secret was to get off the road as soon as possible and as I knew where all the openings in the hedges and the gaps in the walls were, I could be in that other wild, parallel world of nature in minutes. The smell of wet heather wafts and mingles with the sweet aroma of the open countryside and the stillness seems to envelop all. I would pause and listen for the caws of the crows atop the branches of a sprawling oak tree or the melodic song of a goldfinch as he called his mate from a patch of thistles. Sometimes, a startled rabbit, scared by a wily fox, would dart out from beneath a tangle of gorse bushes, his large brown eyes wide with fear as he ran for safety. Off in the distance the faint lowing of grazing cows could be heard if I stopped and was perfectly still. Then the quiet would descend again, dropping slowly. Later that night I asked my father about the rock. He settled in his favorite armchair, rolled a cigarette from his tobacco tin and with smoke curling up toward the ceiling, in a hushed, almost reverent voice, he related the story.

The rock had been placed there soon after the Penal Law was enacted in Ireland in 1607. This law was imposed in retaliation for two major events that occurred earlier. The first was the failed Gunpowder plot of 1605 in which a group of English Catholics tried to blow up the Houses of Parliament in London. The second event took place in early 1607 when a group of Irish noblemen left for Europe to enlist Catholic aid for another revolt against the English crown. This became known as the Flight of the Earls. The Penal law was enacted by the newly crowned King of England and Ireland James I. James, the son of Mary Queen of Scots, was among many other accomplishments, a noted and prolific author, widely known for compiling two important books; the King James version of the bible and a guide book on the subject of witchcraft and how to identify witches, titled Daemonologie. The pilgrims would bring copies of these writings with them to the new world and use them with terrifying results, in Salem, Mass.

The Penal law was strictly enforced by most notably, the Puritan Oliver Cromwell who invaded Ireland in 1649 with his new Model Army, and proceeded to subdue the population with a series of violent, repressive military campaigns. The hope was that within one generation, Catholicism would be eradicated. After the 1641 rebellion, Ireland was under the control of the Irish Confederate Catholics and an alliance was formed with the English Royalists led by the charismatic Charles II the son of Charles I, who had been executed for supposed treason. The law took away all rights from Catholics and effectively banished Bishops. Priests were required to register to preach after this date, but few obeyed this law as it would require an oath of allegiance to the English crown, if they refused were deemed guilty of high treason and faced death, or at best, exile.

Always, an isolated location with a commanding view of the surrounding area would be chosen and a rock taken most times from a demolished Church would be placed there. It would have a simple cross carved on top, consecrated and at that precise moment, become a Mass Rock. The faithful would huddle there in silence, usually at night, rain or shine, fearful and ever watchful for the appearance of the authorities. Their faith was all that sustained them. The dreaded Priest Hunters scoured the countryside hoping to collect the bounty placed on the head of every Priest. My father went on to explain that what all those people wanted to do was to gather there in honor of some man from a place called Galilee who had sacrificed himself for the greater good of mankind. I was convinced that Galilee was somewhere up the Creamery road, but I swear, in all the rambling I did, I never found it there.

Lookouts would be posted to warn of any patrols approaching and when the all clear was given, the Priest would make his appearance and wearing a veil, say Mass. The faithful would respond in whispers and fear would be dominant. If he was ever caught performing this secret ritual, he was executed on the spot. The veil hopefully ensured that he could not be identified by anyone should they be questioned. Thankfully, the Penal Law was abolished in the latter part of the 1800's. Many of these Mass Rocks survive and still dot the Irish landscape today. They serve as a constant reminder of those dark and frightening times and attest to the indomitable and undaunted, Irish spirit.

Chapter 10
Death and Destruction

1   Charles I

Charles I was king of the three kingdoms of England, Scotland, and Ireland from March 1625 until his death in 1649. He was the second son of King James VI of Scotland, but when James ascended the English and Irish thrones in 1603, Charles went to live in England, where he spent much of the rest of his life. His religious policies, together with his marriage to a Roman Catholic, generated animosity among the Puritans, who felt that his beliefs and practices were too Catholic. Charles incurred the wrath of his ministers when he demanded that Parliament increase the tax threshold. When his request was refused, Charles abolished Parliament and set out to rule the kingdom on his own. Finding little support from the people and with his coffers empty, he was left with no choice, and in 1640, he re-convened Parliament.

From 1642, Charles fought continuously with the Scottish and English armies in what came to be known as the English Civil War. He was eventually forced to surrender in 1645, and was handed over to the English army. Charles refused to accept his captors' demands for a constitutional monarchy, and temporarily escaped captivity in November 1647. Re-captured and imprisoned on the Isle of Wight, Charles forged an alliance with Scotland, but by the end of 1648 Oliver Cromwell's New Model Army had consolidated its control over England. Charles was tried, convicted, and executed for high treason in January 1649. The monarchy was abolished and a republic called the 'Commonwealth of England' was declared. England, now without a monarch, became a quasi-republic for the next eleven years. From 1653 to 1658 it was ruled by the Puritan, Oliver Cromwell, whose new title, 'Lord Protector of the Commonwealth of England', came to symbolize fear, violence and extreme cruelty towards anyone perceived as an enemy of the state.

2   Oliver Cromwell

Oliver Cromwell was an English military and political leader and the Lord Protector of the Commonwealth of England, Scotland, and Ireland. He was born in April 1599 and his father, Thomas Cromwell, was a minister in King Henry VIII's court. For the first forty years he led a fairly unimportant existence and only came to prominence after undergoing a religious conversion in the 1630s. As a Puritan, and fanatically religious, Cromwell firmly believed that God was guiding him. In 1628 he was elected Member of Parliament for Huntingdon and Cambridge in 1640 and took part in the English Civil War on the side of the 'Roundheads,' otherwise known as 'Parliamentarians.' He got the nickname 'Old Ironsides,' after he was promoted to commander of the New Model Army.

Cromwell was one of the signatories of Catholic King Charles I's death warrant in 1649, and he dominated the Commonwealth of England as a member of the 'Rump Parliament' between the years 1649–53. The Parliament had long term plans to re-conquer Ireland since 1641, and had already sent an exploratory invasion force to the Island in 1647. Cromwell's hatred towards the Irish was religious as well as political and he was passionately opposed to the Catholic Church. He believed that the Roman Church was heretical and a stumbling block to the Church of England's expansion. He held the Pope and the Catholic church solely responsible for the persecution of Protestants throughout the rest of Europe.

His hatred of Catholicism became an obsession after the Irish Rebellion of 1641 took place. The rebellion was supposed to be bloodless, but became an outright massacre of English and Scottish Protestant settlers by an Irish army comprised of Gaelic chiefs, Old English settlers disloyal to the crown, and clans of Scottish Catholics living in Ireland. The settlers had moved onto the lands taken earlier from Catholic owners to make way for the non-native Protestant planters and these factors contributed to the savagery of the Cromwell military campaign in Ireland. Cromwell was further incensed when in 1649 an alliance was signed by Irish Confederate Catholics and English royalists, who owed their allegiance to Catholic King Charles. Parliament considered the Confederate-Royalist alliance to be the biggest single threat facing the Commonwealth.

Cromwell led an invasion of Ireland, and landed in Dublin on 15 August 1649 with his New Model Army comprised of 12,000 troops. His nine-month military campaign was brief, violent and effective, though it did not end the war in Ireland. Before his invasion, English forces held only small outposts in Dublin and Derry but by the time Cromwell left Ireland, they occupied most of the eastern and northern parts of the country. After his landing at Dublin, Cromwell quickly overwhelmed the towns of Drogheda and Wexford. At the Siege of Drogheda in September 1649, his troops slaughtered almost 3,500 people after capturing the town. Among the fatalities were 2,700 Royalist soldiers, anyone caught carrying arms, large numbers of civilians, prisoners and Roman Catholic priests. Cromwell wrote afterwards, "I am persuaded that this is a righteous judgment of God upon these barbarous wretches, who have imbrued their hands in so much innocent blood and that it will tend to prevent the effusion of blood for the future, which are satisfactory grounds for such actions, which otherwise cannot but work remorse and regret."

After the taking of Drogheda, Cromwell sent a column to Ulster to secure the north of the country and then went on to besiege Waterford, Kilkenny and Clonmel. Kilkenny surrendered on terms, as did many other towns like New Ross and Carlow, but Cromwell failed to take Waterford, and at the siege of Clonmel in May 1650 he lost as many as 2,000 men in abortive assaults before the town surrendered. At the Siege of Wexford in October, another massacre took place under confused circumstances. While Cromwell was apparently trying to negotiate surrender terms, some of his soldiers broke into the town, killed 2,000 Irish troops and up to 1,500 civilians, and burned much of the town. No disciplinary actions were ever taken against his forces after this second massacre. The English conquest of Ireland lasted for a further three years after Cromwell's departure.

The campaigns under his successors Henry Ireton and Edmund Ludlow, consisted of long sieges of fortified cities, towns and villages, coupled with guerrilla warfare in the countryside. Galway, the final Catholic-held town, surrendered in April 1652 and the last Irish Catholic troops surrendered in April 1653. In the wake of the conquest, the public practice of Catholicism was banned and Catholic priests were executed. Dreaded Priest-hunters scoured the land in search of those who were still in hiding and collected the bounties placed on their heads when they turned them over to the authorities. All Catholic-owned land was confiscated under the Settlement of Ireland Act of 1652 and given to Scottish and English settlers, England's financial creditors and Parliamentary soldiers. The remaining Catholic landowners were allocated poorer land in the west of Ireland. During this period, a further series of Penal Laws were passed against Roman Catholics and more of their land was confiscated. Cromwell also led a campaign against the Scottish army between 1650 and 1651.

A major problem for Cromwell after the end of the English Civil War, was the fact that most of the soldiers in his armies still had to be paid. With their coffers empty, Parliament had no money to give them, so Cromwell decided to pay them in land. He evicted and then forcibly moved thousands of the remaining Irish families from their homes in Munster and Leinster and resettled them in counties Clare, Galway, Mayo and Roscommon. This province, known as Connaught, was by far the poorest land in Ireland, except for a three-mile-wide strip of land along the coast. This strip, called the 'Mile Line,' was given to Cromwell's favorite soldiers. The banishment of Catholics to the west of Ireland led to the unpopular phrase, "go to hell or go to Connaught." In 1652 the newly cleared lands in Munster and Leinster were given to Protestants in what was called the 'Cromwellian Settlement.' There was now no part of Ireland where Catholics owned more than half of the land. When he received news that Charles II had landed in Scotland from exile in France and had been proclaimed King, Cromwell left Ireland from Youghal, Cork, on 26 May 1650, to counter the threat. On 20 April 1653, he dismissed the Rump Parliament by force, and set up an assembly known as the 'Barebones Parliament,' before being invited by his fellow leaders to rule as Lord Protector of England, Wales, Scotland and Ireland. As supreme ruler, he maintained an aggressive and effective foreign policy.

Oliver Cromwell died from natural causes in 1658 and was buried in Westminster Abbey. Unable to find a suitable successor for the position of Lord Protector, Parliament reinstated the monarchy with Charles II as King, but this time with drastically reduced power. Charles relaxed the anti-Catholic laws that Cromwell had introduced, but didn't make any attempt to reverse the land confiscations that had taken place in Ireland. He had Cromwell's body exhumed, hung, decapitated and the body thrown in a latrine. His head was placed on a stake where it remained until a storm finally dislodged it more than fifty years later.

3   Charles II

Following the execution of Charles Ist, in January 1649, at the end the English Civil War, his son Charles II was crowned King of Scotland. His short reign as the Scottish monarch lasted from 1649 until his deposition in 1651, In 1660 he was crowned King of England, Scotland, and Ireland, after the monarchy was restored. Charles was popularly known as the 'Merry Monarch,' a reference to both the liveliness of his court and the widespread relief at the return to normality after over a decade of rule by Oliver Cromwell and the Puritans. Although the Parliament of Scotland had proclaimed Charles as King on 5 February 1649, England had entered the period known as the English Commonwealth, and the country became a quasi-republic, led by Oliver Cromwell.

Cromwell had defeated Charles at the Battle of Worcester on 3 September 1651, and forced him to flee to mainland Europe. Cromwell then became dictator of England, Scotland and Ireland, and Charles spent the next nine years in exile in France, the Dutch Republic, and the Spanish Netherlands. A political crisis that followed the death of Cromwell in 1658 resulted in the restoration of the monarchy, and Charles was invited to return to Britain. On 29 May 1660, his 30th birthday, he returned to London amidst public acclaim. After 1660, all legal documents were changed to show that he had succeeded his father as king in 1649. Charles' Parliament enacted laws known as the 'Clarendon Code,' designed to bolster the position of the re-established Church of England. Charles grudgingly agreed to the Code even though he favored a more lenient policy of religious tolerance. An important foreign policy issue during his reign was the threat of the outbreak of the 'Second Anglo-Dutch War.' In 1670, Charles signed the clandestine 'Treaty of Dover,' which forged an alliance with his first cousin King Louis XIV of France. King Louis agreed to aid him in the 'Third Anglo-Dutch War,' and Charles in return promised to convert to Catholicism at a future date. Charles did attempt to introduce religious freedom for Catholics and Protestant dissenters with his 1672 'Royal Declaration of Indulgence,' but his Parliament disagreed and he was forced to withdraw it.

In 1679, revelations surfaced of a supposed "Popish Plot" and sparked the 'Exclusion Crisis' when it was revealed that Charles's brother and heir James, the Duke of York, was a Catholic. The crisis saw the birth of the pro-exclusion Whig and anti-exclusion Tory parties. Charles sided with the Tories, and, following the discovery of the 'Rye House Plot,' a plan to murder Charles and James in 1683, some Whig leaders were executed or forced into exile. Charles dissolved the English Parliament in 1681, and ruled alone until his death on 6 February 1685. He was received into the Roman Catholic Church on his deathbed. Charles II was succeeded by his brother, the Catholic James II.

4   Oliver Plunkett

On January 18 1674, Bishop Oliver Plunkett and his close friend John Brennan, Bishop of Cashel, were forced to flee the town of Drogheda and run for their lives. Wearing long, hooded cloaks and veils, and with a price on their heads and the dreaded Priest Hunters snarling at their heels, they crossed the Boyne valley and fled north toward the sanctuary of South Armagh, in the province of Ulster. In a gale driven, blinding snowstorm they passed in frigid silence through the gap of the north and arrived exhausted in the foothills below the steep slopes of Slieve Gullion. After trudging through the snowdrifts that covered the wide valley of Mullaghbawn, they arrived at a prearranged hiding place known locally as the Doctor's Quarters, close to the old lime kilns at Lislea. There they met with Bishop Patrick Donnelly, aka Phelim Brady, the Bard of Armagh, himself no stranger to the same vicious head hunters. The bard provided the two men with temporary shelter, food and warm beds.

Oliver Plunkett was born on the 1st of November 1625 in Loughcrew, County Meath, Ireland, to well-to-do parents with Hiberno-Norman ancestors. As an aspirant to the priesthood he set out for Rome in 1647, under the care of Father Pierfrancesco Scarampi of the Roman Oratory. At this time the Irish Confederate Wars were raging in Ireland, a series of violent conflicts between native Irish Roman Catholics, English and Irish Anglicans and Protestants. Scarampi was the Papal envoy to the Roman Catholic movement known as the Confederation of Ireland. Many of Plunkett's relatives were involved in this organization. He was admitted to the Irish College in Rome and was ordained a priest in 1654, and deputed by the Irish bishops to act as their representative in Rome. Meanwhile, the Cromwellian conquest of Ireland (1649–53) had defeated the Roman Catholic cause in Ireland and in the aftermath the public practice of Roman Catholicism was banned and Roman Catholic clergy were exiled or executed. As a result, it was impossible for Plunkett to return to Ireland for many years. He petitioned to remain in Rome and, in 1657, became a professor of theology.

Throughout the period of the Commonwealth and the first years of Charles II's reign, he successfully pleaded the cause of the Irish Roman Church, and also served as theological professor at the College of Propaganda Fide. At the Congregation of Propaganda Fide on 9 July 1669 he was appointed Archbishop of Armagh, the Irish primatial see, and was consecrated on 30 November at Ghent by the Bishop of Ghent, Eugeen-Albert, count d'Allamont. He eventually set foot on Irish soil again on 7 March 1670, as the English Restoration of 1660 had begun on a basis of toleration. After arriving back in Ireland, he set about reorganizing the ravaged Roman Church and built schools both for the young and for clergy. As the Penal Laws had been relaxed in line with the Declaration of Breda in 1660, Plunkett was able to establish a Jesuit College in Drogheda in 1670. A year later 150 students attended the college, no fewer than 40 of whom were Protestant, making this college the first integrated school in Ireland.

On the enactment of the Test Act in 1673, to which Plunkett would not agree for doctrinal reasons, the college was closed and demolished. Plunkett went into hiding, travelling only in disguise, and refused a government edict to register at a seaport to await passage into exile. For the next few years he was largely left in peace since the Dublin government, except when put under pressure from the English government in London, preferred to leave the Catholic bishops alone. The so-called Popish Plot, concocted in England by clergyman Titus Oates, led to further anti-Roman Catholic action. Archbishop Peter Talbot of Dublin was arrested, and Plunkett again went into hiding. Despite being on the run and with a price on his head, Plunkett refused to leave his flock. At some point before his final incarceration, he took refuge in a church that once stood in the townland of Killartry, in the parish of Clogherhead in County Louth, seven miles outside Drogheda.

The protestant parliament in England, still in a very strong position, finally forced its will on the restoration King, Charles II, and issued a decree dissolving all Church property. Oliver Plunkett's schools in Drogheda were razed to the ground and a short time later, on the January 18 1674, Oliver Plunkett and his close friend John Brennan, Bishop of Cashel, were forced to flee and seek shelter in the South Armagh hills, coming first to the area around the foothills of Slieve Gullion. This flight is well documented by Oliver Plunkett himself, in a letter written by him to the Internuncio in Rome on January 27 1674 from his first hideout, the house of a 'reduced gentleman who had nothing to lose' and who gave them shelter as they fled, fearing for their lives, through the valleys around Mullaghbawn in County Armagh during a violent snowstorm in the winter of 1673-74.

The man who gave them shelter is believed to be Bishop Patrick Donnelly, also known as Phelim Brady, the Bard of Armagh. Oliver Plunkett was arrested in Dublin in December 1679 and imprisoned in Dublin Castle, where he gave absolution to the dying Talbot. Plunkett was tried at Dundalk for conspiring against the state by allegedly plotting to bring 20,000 French soldiers into the country, and for levying a tax on his clergy to support 70,000 men for rebellion. Fearing he would not be found guilty in Ireland he was moved to Newgate Prison in London in order to face trial at Westminster Hall.

Oliver Plunkett was found guilty of high treason in June 1681 "for promoting the Roman faith", and was condemned to death. He was hanged, drawn and quartered at Tyburn on 1 July 1681, aged 55, the last Roman Catholic martyr to die in England. His body was initially buried in two tin boxes, next to five Jesuits who had died previously, in the courtyard of St Giles in the Fields church. The remains were exhumed in 1683 and moved to the Benedictine monastery at Lamspringe, near Hildesheim in Germany. The head was brought to Rome, and from there to Armagh, and eventually to Drogheda where since 29 June 1921 it has rested in Saint Peter's Church.

Most of the body was brought to Downside Abbey, England, where the major part is located today, with some parts remaining at Lamspringe. Some relics were brought to Ireland in May 1975, while others are in England, France, Germany, the United States, and Australia. On July 1st 1981 South Armagh native Cardinal Tomás Ó Fiaich, together with twenty bishops and a number of abbots stood on a stage beneath a scaffolding on Clapham Common, London. The Cardinal had flown there in a helicopter with the remains of Oliver Plunket's body, for the 300th anniversary of his death and a spectacular rally and Mass was held in his honor.

5   James II

In 1685, James, Duke of York, became King of England, Ireland and Scotland. James was a Catholic and introduced new laws for religious toleration of Catholics and Presbyterians. But when he began promoting Catholics up to the higher ranks of the army, Parliament became suspicious that he was trying to make England an officially Catholic country again. To complicate matters, James' daughter, Mary, married William of Orange and thus William became an heir to the English throne. In 1687, James made William, his brother-in-law, viceroy to Ireland in an attempt to bolster the Irish army in the event that he would soon need their help. The fact that James was a Catholic, made it easier to find recruits in Ireland, but when William attempted to garrison some of the Catholic troops in Derry in 1688, the Protestant inhabitants refused them entry. Nobody was brave enough to tell the troops they were not welcome, however, and eventually it was the young apprentice boys of the city who shut the gates as the troops tried to gain entrance.

Also in 1688, war broke out in Europe after a long series of peace talks broke down. On one side was France, and on the other, the Grand Alliance. The Alliance consisted of Spain, Holland, Germany, Hungary, Naples,

Prussia and Sweden. The Alliance's commander was William of Orange, a Protestant from an estate in the "Orange" region of Holland. Events took another ominous turn in 1688 when James became father to another son. James now considered the new child, born as Catholic, his rightful successor, but Parliament regarded William, a Protestant, as the rightful heir. Fearful that James would try and prevent William from becoming King, Parliament invited William to England to take over the monarchy.

As James's reign was unpopular among the Protestant majority, William, with the support of many important and influential political and religious leaders, invaded England in what became known as the 'Glorious Revolution.' In November 1688, he landed on the south coast of England at the head of a large army and marched on London. James was deposed soon after and William and Mary were crowned as joint sovereigns in his place. William and Mary reigned together until Mary's death in December 1694, after which William ruled as sole monarch. William's reputation as a strong Protestant enabled him to take the British crowns because there was the threat of a revival of Catholicism under James. His reign in England marked the beginning of the transition from the rule of the Stuarts to the more Parliament based rule of the House of Hanover and did not bode well for Ireland.

6   William of Orange

William III, also widely known as 'William of Orange,' was born in The Hague in the Dutch Republic on 4 November 1650. He was the sovereign Prince of Orange and the Stadtholder of Holland, Zeeland, Utrecht, Gelderland, and Overijssel in the Dutch Republic from 1672, and King of England, Ireland, and Scotland from 1689 until his death. As King of Scotland, he was known as William II and is remembered by the Protestant population in Ulster and Scotland as "King Billy." William inherited the House of Orange from his father, William II, who died a week before he was born. His mother Mary, was the daughter of King Charles I of England. In 1677, he wed his fifteen-year-old first cousin Mary, the daughter of his uncle James, Duke of York. William took part in several wars against the powerful Catholic King of France, Louis XIV, and most Protestants revered him as the defender and champion of the true faith.

7   The Battle of the Boyne

Knowing he could rely on Catholic support, King James invaded Ireland in March 1689 as the first step on the road to the recovery of his throne. The protestant inhabitants, who supported William, took up arms and launched a series of attacks against James' new army. Misjudging the strength of James' troops, they were driven back inside the walls of Derry and Enniskillen. James, employing the age old practice of 'siege,' dug in around both towns with the express aim of starving the enemy into submission. A barrier was placed across the River Foyle making it impossible for supply ships to enter and Derry was left without food for almost four months. The siege was finally broken when one of William's ships, the Mountjoy, arrived and smashed through the blockade on 28 July 1689, after which James fled. Companies of James' soldiers who had been sieging Enniskillen, were surrounded and defeated at Newtownbutler, in Fermanagh. In August 1689, William's armies landed in the town of Carrickfergus in Antrim and prepared for a major offensive.

In March 1690, four thousand well-armed Danish troops arrived in Belfast to lend support to William in the belief that doing so would shorten the war in Ireland and allow William's return to fighting in Europe. Frances' King Louis, on the other hand, sent his troops to aid James because he wished to prolong the war in Ireland, so that William's attention would continue to be diverted away from the war in Europe. In June 1690, William, together with a large army, arrived at Carrickfergus, joined forces with the Dutch army and marched south toward Leinster. James marched north from Dublin and the two armies met on the banks of the River Boyne, in Co Meath on 1 July, 1690. The ensuing battle, known as the 'Battle of the Boyne,' is arguably the best remembered event in Irish history, and was the last battle fought on Irish soil, with two opposing Kings actually present on the battlefield.

When the smoke cleared and the dust settled, it was clear that William was the victor having lost as few as four hundred men. In contrast, James, whose casualties numbered more than thirteen hundred, and clearly the loser, was forced to retreat south to Dublin and soon after, he fled to France. William's victory was lauded all across Europe as it was seen as a defeat by the Grand Alliance over France. James' viceroy, General St. Ruth, stayed in Ireland and led the remnants of James' army to attack Limerick and Athlone. He managed to inflict several defeats on William's army with the result that William failed to capture the city of Limerick despite laying siege to it. William returned to England leaving his general Ginkel in charge. Ginkel offered the supporters of James a peace settlement, but they refused and decided to fight on under the leadership of the Marquis St. Ruth.

William's armies further compounded their victory when on the On 12 July, 1691 the two armies met at Aughrim, near Athlone, County Galway. General Ginkel, despite not being in a classic assault position, made the decision to launch an attack anyway and after several bloody skirmishes, routed James' army and won a decisive victory. General St. Ruth was killed in the battle and his surviving troops retreated back to Limerick. On 26 September 1691, James' army surrendered and a peace treaty was signed in October 1691. This became known as the Treaty of Limerick and allowed Catholics to retain the right to practice their religion, but they had to relinquish their property and land holdings. Those who chose to leave Ireland at that time eventually became known as the 'Wild Geese'.

Chapter 11
Resurgence and Emancipation

After the Treaty of Limerick was signed, a further series of Penal Laws were passed by the Irish Parliament. The sole purpose was to continue to rid Ireland of Catholicism, by insisting that Catholics convert to Protestantism. These new laws were so harsh that many Irish did convert in an attempt to escape the penalties that were incurred by those who broke the Laws. But Catholics were not the only group to be discriminated against. In 1704 a law had been passed which banned Presbyterians from town councils and other official positions, and Presbyterian ministers were further banned from conducting wedding ceremonies. In 1728 a law was passed which banned Catholics from voting. Another one introduced stated that if a man converted to Protestantism he would be granted his Catholic family's confiscated property and lands.

1   American Revolution

In 1713, France made peace with England and by signing the Treaty of Utrecht, finally brought an end to the war that had lasted for almost twenty-five years. Now in command of a large, modern naval force, and with Ireland finally subdued, England felt sure that they were in a strong position to explore, conquer and exploit foreign territories. During the 18th century, colonization was the by-word and England set in place its plan for expansion.

In rapid succession they invaded India, Africa, Australia and the Americas. The era of the 'British Empire' had dawned, but as history shows, war was always their constant companion. In 1776, England went to war with the colonists who lived in towns along the east coast of America. The colonists, after a series of harsh taxes were imposed by King George III on all imports and exports, rebelled against the crown and took up arms in defense of their homes and way of life. Despite fighting a war that lasted almost ten years, England lost control of its New England colonies in 1777 and signed a treaty. The Treaties of Paris, in which England finally recognized the independence of the American states and returned Florida to Spain, were signed in 1782 and 1783.

2   Louis XVI of France

Louis XVI was King of France from 1774 until his deposition in 1792. The first part of his reign was marked by attempts to reform France in accordance with the 'Enlightenment' ideas popular at that time. These included efforts to abolish serfdom and increase tolerance toward non-Catholics. The French nobility reacted to the proposed reforms with hostility, and successfully opposed their implementation. Louis deregulated the grain market, as advised by his minister Turgot, but it resulted in an increase in the price of flour. In times of bad harvests, it would lead to food scarcity and eventually prompt the masses to revolt. From 1776 Louis supported the North American colonists in their fight for independence from England, which was achieved with the signing of the Treaty of Paris in 1783.

3   French Revolution

The expense incurred by the financing of wars, foreign and domestic, put a major drain on the country's exchequer, and the financial crisis which ensued contributed greatly to the unpopularity of the French Royal family. Discord among the middle and lower classes resulted in vociferous opposition to the aristocracy in general and the monarchy in particular, of which Louis and his wife, Queen Marie Antoinette, were seen as being the representatives. In 1789, the storming of the Bastille, which occurred during a period of violent rioting in Paris, marked the beginning of the French Revolution. Louis XVI was suspended and arrested on 10 August 1792, one month before the monarchy was abolished and the First French Republic was proclaimed on 21 September 1792.

Louis XVI was tried by the National Convention, found guilty of high treason, and executed by guillotine on 21 January 1793. Louis was the only French King ever to be executed, and his death brought an end to more than a thousand years of unbroken French monarchy. Out of the mayhem and bloodshed emerged a new French republic, and for many peasants throughout Europe, this new democracy concept was very appealing, since it gave the power to the people. In 1791, the newly installed French government offered military assistance to any group who wished to be rid of their King. This did not bode well for the Royal families of England, Spain, Germany and Austria and war soon broke out between these Kingdoms and France.

4   United Irishmen

In Ireland at this time a new organization was formed. With a leader named Theobald Wolfe Tone, the organization, called the United Irishmen, was comprised of both Presbyterians and Catholics. Their manifesto declared the belief in a peaceful future for Ireland in which all could live together in harmony and equality. They wanted to set up a French-styled democratic republic, which was to be completely free and independent of England. They quickly gained countrywide support, although many were vehemently opposed to their principles, especially the newly formed Orange Order in Ulster, which set out to preserve loyalty to the English monarchy.

England, being a constitutional monarchy, believed that anyone who supported the new form of French Republicanism espoused by the United Irishmen, was guilty of treason and declared the organization illegal. The English already regarded themselves as democratic and therefore viewed the United Irishmen as a national threat to be stamped out. Early in 1798, the English authorities began attacking known United Irishmen, and murdered large numbers of Presbyterian and Catholic members. Wolfe Tone realized that if there was going to be a rebellion, it would have to be then before the British destroyed them. So the rebellion was planned and began in the spring of 1798, in Down, Antrim and Wexford. Several bloody battles took place at Antrim, Ballynahinch and Saintfield and the United Irishmen were finally defeated at the Battle of Vinegar Hill in Wexford.

Not everything was lost however, because in late 1798, the French government sent troops and provisions to support Tone. They landed in Mayo, quickly gained local support, took over the area and marched north. After a series of bloody battles with many casualties on both sides, the United Irishmen were defeated at a decisive battle in Sligo. The French troops were taken prisoner but the surviving Irish soldiers were massacred as a punishment for treason.

Although the rebellion had been put down, it was clear that Republicanism in Ireland could not be ignored and serious changes were needed in the way Ireland was governed to ensure that such violence did not occur again. Wolfe Tone committed suicide in prison whilst awaiting execution.

5   The Act of Union

In 1800, England passed an Act of Union. The act essentially formed a new country and came to be known as 'The United Kingdom of Great Britain and Ireland' commonly called the 'United Kingdom.' This meant that England, Wales, Ireland and Scotland were now united and a new flag was unfurled. The flag, made up of parts of the flags of each former country, was called the Union Jack. All other parliaments were disbanded and from then on the United Kingdom would be ruled from a single parliament in London. For most Irish, there wasn't a noticeable difference, but it meant that Irish government representatives could not pass laws on their own.

6   Daniel O'Connell

The hated penal laws were still in force in Ireland in the early 1800s and continued to discriminate against Catholics, Presbyterians and Dissenters, despite earlier promises that they would be abolished with the Act of Union. However, this did not happen and it took the actions of Daniel O'Connell to lead a campaign for emancipation that captured the public's imagination and led to the necessary legislation being passed in 1829. In 1800 the population of Ireland was between 4 and 5 million, with 200,000 living in Dublin. However, the burgeoning Industrial revolution and especially the expansion of the Irish Linen industry in the first half of the century allowed the population to grow dramatically.

Daniel O'Connell was born at Carhan near Caherciveen, County Kerry, to the O'Connells of Derrynane, a once-wealthy Roman Catholic family, that had been dispossessed of its lands. Among his uncles was Daniel Charles, Count O'Connell, an officer in the Irish Brigades of the French Army. O'Connell studied at Douai in France and was admitted as a barrister to Lincoln's Inn in 1794, transferring to Dublin's King's Inn two years later. In his early years, he became acquainted with the pro-democracy radicals of the time and committed himself to peacefully bringing equal rights and religious tolerance to his own country.

While in Dublin studying law, O'Connell was under his Uncle Maurice's instructions not to become involved in any militia activity. When Wolfe Tone's French invasion fleet entered Bantry Bay in December 1796, O'Connell found himself in a quandary. Dennis Gwynn in his biography 'Daniel O'Connell: The Irish Liberator' suggests that O'Connell was worried because he was enrolled as a volunteer in defense of Government, yet the same Government was blatantly repressing the Catholic people. O'Connell's studies at the time had concentrated upon the legal and political history of Ireland, and he was fully aware of this as he stated, "in Ireland the whole policy of the Government is to repress the people and to maintain the ascendancy of a privileged and corrupt minority." On 3 January 1797, he wrote to his uncle saying that he was the last of his colleagues to join a volunteer corps and "being young, active, healthy and single," he could offer no plausible excuse. Later that month he joined the Lawyer's Artillery Corps.

On 19 May 1798, O'Connell was called to the Irish Bar and became a barrister. Four days later, the United Irishmen staged their rebellion which was put down by the British with great bloodshed. As a peace loving man, O'Connell, a committed pacifist, did not support the rebellion as he believed that the Irish would have to assert themselves politically rather than by force. He also condemned Robert Emmet's Rebellion of 1803. Of Emmet, who was a Protestant, he wrote: "A man who could coolly prepare so much bloodshed, so many murders and such horrors of every kind has ceased to be an object of compassion." Despite his opposition to the use of violence, he was willing to defend those accused of political crimes, particularly if he suspected that they had been falsely accused, as in the Doneraile conspiracy trials of 1829, his last notable Court appearance. In 1811, O'Connell established the Catholic Board, which fought for Catholic emancipation, and the opportunity for Irish Catholics to become members of parliament. In 1823, he set up the Catholic Association which embraced other aims to aid Irish Catholics, such as, electoral reform, reform of the Church of Ireland, tenants' rights, and economic development. The Association was funded by membership dues of one penny per month, a small amount designed to attract Catholic peasants. The subscription was highly successful, and the Association raised a large sum of money in its first year. The money was used to campaign for Catholic emancipation, and the funding of pro-emancipation members of parliament, who were standing for the British House of Commons.

7   The Great Hunger of 1847

By 1841, there were 8,175,000 people living in Ireland, eighty percent of whom were poverty stricken. Most Irish landlords were Protestants, simply because the law forbade Catholics from owning land. The Irish peasants, as they were called, were comprised of both Presbyterian and Catholic, and lived in desperate conditions. Living and farming as they did, on land owned by the notorious 'Absentee Landlords,' they had to pay rent which was collected by an agent appointed by the landlord. Many of those 'agents' were notoriously dis-honest and often abused their positions by charging more than the agreed amount of rent, then pocketed the difference. If a tenant could not afford to pay the rent in cash, property, including livestock and crops, would be taken in lieu.

In 1815 a series of measures were introduced throughout the United Kingdom, which placed restrictions and tariffs on all imported grain. The 'Corn Laws' as they became known, were designed to keep grain prices high in favor of the landowners and ensure the continuation of large profits. 'The Corn Laws' imposed high import taxes, which made it too costly to import grain from abroad, even when food supplies were scarce. Food prices soared as a direct result of the 'Corn Law' and in Ireland, the only locally grown crop that could be relied on was the potato. In 1845 a fungal disease called 'phytophthora infestans', or 'potato blight' struck and wiped out a third of the potato crop in Ireland, a disaster for the ordinary people who relied upon it.

Those who lived near towns were better off, since towns had other sources of food, but things got desperate for those living in the countryside. By 1846, supplies of stored potatoes had sold out and many people began to starve slowly. Sadly, the crop of 1846 also failed and this time wiped out almost all the potatoes in Ireland. Thousands of people starved, particularly in rural areas with untold numbers dying from typhus, scurvy and dysentery. Tens of thousands of corpses lay along the roadsides, their mouths turned green from eating grass in desperation, which led to the term the 'green mouth death.' The problem was made worse by cold-hearted landlords who evicted families who could not pay their rent because they had no potatoes left to sell. Fortunately, the crop of 1847 was good, and, although the crop of 1848 also failed, the starvation was not as bad as it was in 1846. Many thousands decided to cut their losses and set sail on emigration ships to America. Thousands died on the ships, which were so overcrowded that they became known as 'coffin ships'. By 1851, the population had fallen twenty-five percent to 6,000,000 and the emigrations continued until around 1900, by which time only 4,500,000 remained in Ireland. This caused large areas of land to be abandoned and today, large swathes of derelict farmland can be seen in Counties Mayo and Galway.

Many people believed that the British could have done more and this caused a lot of anti-British sentiment to arise in Ireland and among the Irish who had gone to America. The horrible fact that people starved to death while cattle, sheep and grain continued to be exported, sometimes under military escort, caused deep-seated bitterness and long-lasting resentment among the survivors. The huge numbers of emigrants caused by the food shortages also ensured that such feelings were not confined to Ireland, but spread to England, the United States, Australia, and all other countries where Irish emigrants now lived. Shocked by the scenes of starvation and greatly influenced by the revolutions breaking out all across Europe, a small group of agitators known as the 'Young Irelanders' moved toward armed insurrection. In 1848 an attempted uprising failed after several countrywide incidents and a violent skirmish in Ballingary, Co Tipperary were quickly and violently put down. The government rounded up many of the participants and imprisoned them. Those not captured fled the country and their supporters disbanded.

8   The Fenians

During the latter part of 1866, money was raised in America for a new rebellion that was to occur in 1867. This 'Fenian Rising' was badly organized, had little support and many of the organizers were arrested when they landed in Cork. Minor flare ups across the country were soon put down by the police and army. On 22 November 1867 three Fenians, William Philip Allen, Michael O'Brian, and Michael Larkin known as the Manchester Martyrs, were executed in Salford for their attack on a police van to release Fenians held captive earlier that year. On 13 December 1867 the Fenians exploded a bomb in an effort to free one of their members being held on remand at Clerkenwell Prison in London.

The explosion damaged nearby houses, killed twelve people and injured one hundred and twenty. None of the prisoners escaped and the bombing was later described as the most infamous action carried out by the Fenians in Great Britain in the 19th century. It enraged the public, causing a backlash of hostility in Britain which undermined efforts to establish home rule or independence for Ireland. In 1882, a breakaway IRB faction calling itself the Irish 'National Invincibles' assassinated the British Chief Secretary for Ireland, Lord Frederick Cavendish and his secretary, in an incident that became known as the 'Phoenix Park Murders.' In March 1883 the London Metropolitan Police's Special Irish Branch was formed, to monitor the 'Invincibles' activity.

9 Irish Republican Brotherhood

In 1858 a new group calling themselves the Irish Republican Brotherhood was formed with the aim of creating an independent Irish republic by force. Unlike previous groups, the IRB had a large support base, particularly from the Irish who had gone to America. In 1867 they staged an uprising but it was easily defeated by the British. The Fenians, a militant arm of the IRB, went into the background for the next thirty years, but still existed. The IRB was the first group to add a religious slant to Republicanism, and this widened the gap between the two religious groups who shared Ireland. The Irish Republican Brotherhood (IRB) was a secret oath-bound fraternal organization dedicated to the establishment of an "independent democratic republic."

In Ireland between 1858 and 1924. Its counterpart in the United States of America was organized by John O'Mahony and became known as the Fenian Brotherhood (later Clan na Gael). The members of both wings of the movement are often referred to as "Fenians". The IRB played an important role in the history of Ireland, as the chief advocate of republicanism during the campaign for Ireland's independence from the United Kingdom, successor to movements such as the United Irishmen of the 1790s and the Young Irelanders of the 1840s.

Early in 1900 the Irish Republican Brotherhood (IRB) was a shadow of its former self and more concerned with local political issues rather than armed rebellion. This was all about to change however, with the founding of the "Dungannon Clubs" in Ulster. The clubs were set up initially to deter anyone wishing to join the British Army, and instead, encouraged signing up to the IRB, whose aim now was total independence from Britain and the formation of an Irish Republic. In 1909 a young man named Michael Collins was introduced to the brotherhood by member Sam Maguire. Collins would eventually go down in the annals of Irish history as one of the toughest individuals in the fight for Irish freedom.

The IRB staged the Easter Rising in 1916, which led to the establishment of the first Dáil Éireann in 1919. After the collapse of the 1848 rebellion James Stephens and John O'Mahony went to Europe to avoid arrest. In Paris they supported themselves through teaching and translation work and planned the next stage of "the fight to overthrow British rule in

Ireland." Stephens in Paris, set himself three tasks, during his seven years of exile. They were, to keep alive, pursue knowledge, and master the technique of conspiracy.

Chapter 12
War and Insurrection

1   Home Rule Bill

As the 20th century dawned, an old monster reared its ugly head once again. The monster, in the form of a third 'Home Rule Bill' was re-introduced in 1912 and stayed on the table until 1918. The Irish Home Rule movement promoted self-government for Ireland and was the most important political movement of Irish nationalism, from 1870 to the end of World War I. In 1870, Isaac Butt founded the 'Home Government Association.' It was succeeded in 1873 by the 'Home Rule League' and by 1882 it was known as the 'Irish Parliamentary Party.' These organizations fought for home rule for Ireland in the British House of Commons. Under the leadership of Charles Stewart Parnell, the movement came close to success when William Gladstone's' Liberal government, introduced the First 'Home Rule Bill' in 1886, but it was defeated in the House of Commons after a split in the Liberal Party occurred. After Parnell's death, Gladstone introduced the 'Second Home Rule Bill' in 1893, which passed in the House of Commons but was turned down in the House of Lords. After the removal of the House of Lords' veto in 1911, the 'Third Home Rule Bill' was introduced in 1912, and sparked the Home Rule Crisis.

In 1912 a group calling themselves the 'Ulster Volunteers' was formed with the express purpose of resisting, by force, any notion of Home Rule. The IRB responded in kind and formed the 'Irish Volunteers' in November

1913. Though the Volunteers' purpose was not the establishment of a Republic, they eventually would use the organization to do just that. From the outset they set out to recruit high-ranking members into their ranks, men such as Joseph Plunkett, Thomas MacDonagh, and Patrick Pearse, who would later lead the Supreme Council in 1915. These men, together with Tom Clarke, Sean MacDermott, Eamonn Ceannt and eventually James Connolly of the Irish Citizen Army, made up the Military Committee, the organizers and leaders of the Rising of 1916.

2   Easter Rebellion 1916

On Easter Monday, 24 April 1916, Patrick Pearse, together with members of the Irish Volunteers, the Irish Citizen Army, led by James Connolly, and two hundred women of Cumann na mBan, seized key government buildings in Dublin and at four minutes past noon, declared their establishment of an Irish Republic. The British Army brought in thousands of troops, heavy artillery and a gunboat made its way up the river Liffey to the center of the city. Fierce battles broke out in the streets and alleyways all around Dublin, especially on the roads leading into the city. The rebels put up stiff resistance, slowing the British advance and inflicting heavy casualties. Elsewhere in Dublin, the fighting mainly consisted of sniping and long-range gun battles. The main rebel positions were slowly surrounded and bombarded with artillery.

In other parts of the country there were isolated actions, with attacks on the Royal Irish Constabulary (RIC) barracks at Ashbourne, County Meath and in County Galway. The rebels managed to overrun and capture the town of Enniscorthy, County Wexford, but the fiercest fighting took place in Dublin City. An eagerly awaited arms shipment from Germany had been intercepted just before the Rising began, prompting one of the Volunteer leaders, Eoin MacNeill to issue a countermanding order in an attempt to halt the Rising. This caused confusion and reduced the number of rebels who eventually took part. With greater numbers and superior weapons, the British Army suppressed the Rising. Patrick Pearse agreed to an unconditional surrender on Saturday 29 April, although fighting continued until Sunday, when word reached the other rebel positions. After the surrender the country remained under martial law. About three thousand five hundred people were taken prisoner by the British, many of whom had played no part in the Rising, and one thousand eight hundred of them were sent to internment camps or prisons in Britain. Most of the leaders of the Rising were executed following a series of hastily held military trials. Almost five hundred people were killed in the Easter Rising with about fifty-four percent civilians, thirty percent British military and police, and sixteen percent Irish rebels. More than two thousand six hundred were wounded. Many of the civilians were killed as a result of the British using artillery and heavy machine guns, or mistaking civilians for rebels, many others were caught in crossfires. The shelling and the firestorm that ensued ravaged the city and smoldered for weeks leaving many parts of the inner city in ruins.

3   War of Independence

The Irish War of Independence or Anglo-Irish War was a guerrilla war fought from 1919 to 1921 between the Irish Republican Army (IRA,) and the British security forces in Ireland. In the December 1918 election, the Irish Republican party, Sinn Féin (ourselves alone) won a landslide political victory in Ireland. The victory was a direct popular response to the executions of the signatories of the Irish Proclamation which had been read on the steps of the General Post Office, by Patrick Pearse in April 1916 at the start of the rebellion. On January 21, 1919 Sinn Fein formed a government (Dáil Éireann) and declared independence from Britain. Later that day, two members of the armed police force, the Royal Irish Constabulary (RIC) were shot dead in County Tipperary by IRA members acting on their own initiative. The war of Independence had begun.

For much of 1919, IRA activity included procurement of weapons and the freeing of republican prisoners. In September the British government outlawed both the Dáil and Sinn Féin, and the war escalated soon after. The IRA began attacking RIC and British Army patrols, assaulting their barracks and forcing isolated police stations to be abandoned. The British government bolstered the RIC with raw, badly trained recruits from Britain called the Black and Tans who were notorious for ill-discipline and savage reprisal attacks on civilians. Around three hundred people were killed in the conflict, and by late 1920 there was a major upsurge in violence. On Sunday, 21 November 1920, a day that became known as 'Bloody Sunday,' fourteen

British intelligence agents, known as the 'Cairo Gang' were assassinated in Dublin in the early morning.

Later in the afternoon of the same day, the RIC opened fire on a crowd at a football match in the city, killing fourteen civilians and wounding sixty-five. One week later, seventeen Black and Tans were killed by the IRA in an ambush at Kilmichael in County Cork. As a result of this violent upsurge the British government declared martial law in much of southern Ireland and Cork City was burned by British forces in December 1920. Violence continued to escalate over the next seven months, and one thousand people were killed and four thousand five hundred republicans interned. The fighting was heaviest in Munster particularly Cork, and there was heavy fighting in both Dublin and Belfast. These three areas bore the brunt with over seventy-five percent of the fatalities. Violence in Ulster, particularly Belfast, was notable for its sectarian character and the high number of Catholic civilian victims.

Britain passed a 'Fourth Home Rule Bill' called the Government of Ireland Act, in 1920, with the intention of creating separate parliaments for Northern and Southern Ireland. The Northern Parliament at Stormont was established in 1921, but it's Southern counterpart never functioned. Following a Treaty that ended the Anglo-Irish War, the 26 southern counties of Ireland gained independence and became known as the Irish Free State.

4   Anglo Irish Treaty

Both sides agreed to a truce on 11 July 1921 and in May, Ireland was partitioned by an Act of the British Parliament. The act created the state called 'Northern Ireland,' this despite the fact that Counties Fermanagh, Tyrone, Derry City and most border areas had voted by a majority, for nationalist candidates in the 1918 General Election. The post-ceasefire talks led to the signing of the Anglo-Irish Treaty in London in December 1921. This treaty ended British rule in twenty-six counties of Ireland and the Irish Free State was created as a self-governing entity in December 1922. However, the six north-eastern counties remained within the United Kingdom and after the ceasefire, political and sectarian violence between Catholic republicans and protestant loyalists continued un-abated.

The split caused by the signing of the treaty was deeply personal. Many of the leaders on both sides had been close family members, friends and comrades during the War of Independence. This made their disagreement over the treaty all the more bitter. Michael Collins later said that Eamon de Valera had sent him as a scapegoat to negotiate the treaty because he knew that the British would not concede an independent Irish republic and wanted Collins to take the blame for the compromise settlement. He said that he felt deeply betrayed when de Valera refused to stand by the agreement that the Irish delegation had negotiated with David Lloyd George and Winston Churchill. De Valera, for his part, was furious that Collins and Arthur Griffith had signed the treaty without consulting him or the Irish cabinet as instructed.

5   Irish Civil War

The Irish Republican Army (Óglaigh na hEireann) was an Irish republican revolutionary military organization. It was descended directly from the Irish Volunteers, an organization established on 25 November 1913 that staged the Easter Rising in April 1916. In 1919, the Irish Republic that had been proclaimed during the Easter Rising was formally established by an elected assembly (Dáil Éireann), and the Irish Volunteers were recognised by Dáil Éireann as its legitimate army. Thereafter, the IRA waged a guerrilla campaign against the British occupation of Ireland in the 1919–21 Irish War of Independence.

When the Anglo-Irish Treaty was signed on 6 December 1921, it was debated by the Supreme Council, which voted to accept it by eleven votes to four. Dáil Éireann passed the Anglo-Irish Treaty by a margin of sixty-four votes to fifty-seven on 7 January 1922. Upon the Treaty's ratification, Eamon de Valera resigned as President of the Republic and failed to be re-elected by an even closer vote of sixty to fifty-eight. He challenged the right of the Dáil to approve the treaty, saying that its members were breaking their oath to the Irish Republic. The anti-Treaty IRA formed their own "Army Executive", which they declared to be the real government of the country, despite the result of the 1921 general election.

On 14 April 1922, 200 Anti-Treaty IRA militants, led by Rory O'Connor, occupied the Four Courts and several other buildings in central Dublin, resulting in a tense stand-off. The aim was to start a new armed confrontation with the British, which they hoped would unite the two factions of the IRA against their common enemy. However, for those who were determined to turn the Free State into a viable, self-governing Irish state, this was an act of rebellion that would have to be put down by them rather than the British. Sinn Fein leader Arthur Griffith was in favor of using force against these men immediately.

Michael Collins, who wanted at all costs to avoid civil war, left the Four Courts garrison alone until late June 1922. By this point, the Pro-Treaty Sinn Féin party had secured a large majority in the general election, along with other parties that supported the Treaty. Collins was also coming under continuing pressure from London to assert his government's authority in Dublin. The British lost patience as a result of an action which may have been secretly ordered by Collins. It is thought that he had Henry Hughes Wilson, a retired British Army field marshal and a prominent security advisor to the Prime Minister of Northern Ireland James Craig, assassinated in London on 22 June because of his role in the North of Ireland. Winston Churchill assumed that the Anti-Treaty IRA were responsible for the killing and warned Collins that he would use British troops to attack the Four Courts unless the Provisional Government took action. The final straw for the Free State government came on 26 June, when the Four Courts republican garrison kidnapped JJ "Ginger" O'Connell, a general in the new National Army. Collins, after giving the Four Courts garrison a final ultimatum to leave the building on 27 June, decided to end the stand-off by bombarding the garrison into surrender. The government then appointed Collins as Commander-in-Chief of the National Army.

Collins ordered acceptance of the British offer of two pieces of artillery for use by the new army of the Free State. The anti-treaty forces in the Four Courts, who possessed only small arms, surrendered after two days of bombardment and the storming of the building by Provisional Government troops in June 1922). Shortly before the surrender, a massive explosion destroyed the western wing of the complex, including the Irish Public Record Office, injuring many advancing Free State soldiers and destroying the records. Government supporters alleged that the building had been deliberately mined. Pitched battles continued in Dublin until 5 July, as Anti-Treaty IRA units from the Dublin Brigade, led by Oscar Traynor, occupied O'Connell Street, provoking more street fighting which cost both sides sixty-five killed and two hundred and eighty wounded. When the fighting in Dublin died down, the Free State government was left firmly in control of the Irish capital and the anti-treaty forces dispersed around the country, mainly to the south and west.

6   Aftermath

Michael Collins, commander of the Free State's National Army, had hoped for a speedy reconciliation of the warring Irish nationalist factions, demanding that Republicans must accept the people's verdict and then could go home without their arms... "We want to avoid any possible unnecessary destruction and loss of life. We do not want to mitigate their weakness by resolute action beyond what is required." However, following the death of Collins in an ambush on 22 August 1922, the Free State government, under the new leadership of W. T. Cosgrave, Richard Mulcahy and Kevin O'Higgins, took the position that the Anti-Treaty IRA were conducting an unlawful rebellion against the legitimate Irish government and should be treated as criminals rather than as combatants.

O'Higgins in particular voiced the opinion that the use of martial law and executions was the only way to bring the war to an end. Another factor contributing to the executions policy was the escalating level of violence. In the first two months of the Civil War, Free State forces had successfully taken all the territory held by Republicans and the war seemed all but over. After the Anti-Treaty side resorted to guerrilla tactics in August–September, National Army casualties mounted and they even lost control over some of the territory taken in the Irish Free State offensive. On 27 September 1922, three months after the outbreak of war, the Free State's Provisional Government put before the Dáil the Army Emergency Powers Resolution, proposing legislation for setting up military courts. The legislation, commonly referred to as the Public Safety Bill, empowered military tribunals with the ability to impose life imprisonment, as well as the death penalty, for a variety of offences. By imposing capital punishment for anyone found in possession of either firearms or ammunition, the Free State effectively prevented Republican forces from storing arms or ammunition that could be used by them in military operations. Anyone arrested in possession of even a single sporting or civilian firearm, could be summarily executed by firing squad. Offences covered under the law not only included attacks on state policy or military forces, but also the publication of 'seditious documents' as well as membership of the Irish Republican Army. From November 1922, the Free State government embarked on a policy of executing Republican prisoners in order to bring the war to an end.

Many of those killed had previously been allies, and in some cases close friends of those who ordered their deaths in the civil war. In addition, government troops summarily executed prisoners in the field on many occasions. The executions of prisoners left a legacy of bitterness in Irish politics that lasts to the present day. Kevin O'Higgins, the man Republicans saw as most directly responsible for the enactment of the Public Safety Act, with its approval of executions, himself fell victim to assassination by the IRA in 1927, becoming one of the last victims of Civil War era violence in Ireland.

As a result of the executions in the Civil War, many Republicans would never accept the Free State as a legitimate Irish government, and instead viewed it as a repressive, British-imposed government. This attitude was partially alleviated after 1932, when Fianna Fáil, the party that represented the bulk of the Republican constituency, entered government peacefully and introduced a new Constitution in 1937. The use of execution by the Irish Free State in the Civil War was relatively harsh compared to the recent British record. In contrast with seventy-seven official executions by the Irish Free State government, the British executed only twenty-four IRA volunteers during the 1919–21 conflict.

7   Border Campaigns

    1942-1944

The prime minister of the Irish Free State, Eamon de Valera, complained about the occupation of Irish soil with the arrival of American soldiers in Ulster as part of the war effort against Nazi Germany. This influx of foreign soldiers encouraged the northern command of the IRA, under the auspices of newly appointed commander Hugh McAteer, to reorganize and on 25 March 1942 agree to a new campaign against the British military and war effort in The North of Ireland. Over the first few months of the campaign, a few attacks against the Royal Ulster Constabulary (RUC) in Strabane, Dungannon, and Belfast, resulted in the death of two RUC constables and the wounding of two others.

Six IRA members, including Joe Cahill, were arrested during the Belfast incident and sentenced to death for the murder of one of the constables. A petition signed by around two hundred thousand people calling for mercy was gathered by those calling for a reprieve, and several days before the date of the executions, all but one was commuted. The sole IRA member executed was Tom Williams who was hanged at Crumlim Road gaol, Belfast, on 2 September 1942, which resulted in the IRA stepping up their attacks.

After the bombing of Randalstown RUC station, and more gun attacks against the RUC in parts of West Belfast and along the border area between the North and the Irish Free State, around three hundred and twenty members and suspected members of the IRA, including Hugh McAteer, were arrested all across the North. One noted historian, Bowyer-Bell, reports a total of sixty armed attacks by the IRA in the three months up to December 1942, carried out by the remaining fifty to sixty IRA members still at large. In the first few months of 1943, jail breaks at Crumlin Road and Derry saw twenty-three IRA members, including McAteer, escape. This however failed to inspire a resumption of activity as many of the escapees had crossed the border into County Donegal in the Free State and were subsequently recaptured by the Irish Army. The few others that escaped arrest sought refuge from pursuit rather than resuming their attacks.

IRA northern command units in south Derry, and south Armagh were no longer able to function as required, and contact with units in Counties Cavan and Monaghan started to wane. Bowyer-Bell states of the late 1943 period, that the local commanding officers preferred to avoid arrest, and that anything associated with the IRA such as parades, training, and even meetings ended with fear of internment at the internment camp at the Curragh in Co. Kildare.

By the end of the World War II in 1945, the northern command of the IRA, largely as a result of the stern military response from the Free State, had been reduced to a few wanted men with the North of Ireland entirely free from IRA activity. Richard Mulcahy became the leader of Fine Gael in 1948, but never became Taoiseach because of his role in the Civil War. The Free State officially became the 'Republic of Ireland' in 1949. In June 1959, Eamon De Valera was inaugurated as President of Ireland and was re-elected in aged 84, until 2013 a world record for the oldest elected head of state. At his retirement in 1973 at the age of 90, he was the oldest living head of state in the world.

8   Border Campaigns

1956 – 1962

The idea of campaigns launched from the Republic against the British held North of Ireland, was first proposed by Tom Barry in the 1930s. In 1948 a General Army Convention issued General Order No. 8, which stated that "no armed action whatsoever" was to be taken against the forces of the Republic of Ireland. Under this new policy, IRA volunteers who were caught with arms in the Republic of Ireland were ordered to dump or destroy them and not to take defensive action. In 1954, after an arms raid at Gough Barracks in Armagh, a speaker at the Wolfe Tone commemoration at Bodenstown repeated that IRA policy was directed solely against British forces in Northern Ireland. A campaign (codenamed Operation Harvest) was launched in December 1956 and carried out by the Irish Republican Army (IRA) against targets in the North of Ireland. Although the campaign was ultimately a failure militarily, when it ended in February 1962, it was justified as it had kept the IRA engaged for another generation.

Chronology

Key Events from 1966 to the Present

1966

17 April

Loyalists led by Ian Paisley, a Presbyterian fundamentalist preacher, founded the Ulster Constitution Defence Committee (UCDC) to oppose the civil rights movement. It set up a paramilitary-style wing using the umbrella name the Ulster Protestant Volunteers. (UPV)

21 May

A loyalist group calling itself the Ulster Volunteer Force (UVF) issued a statement declaring war on the Irish Republican Army (IRA). The group claimed to be composed of "heavily armed Protestants dedicated to this cause." At the time, the IRA was not engaged in armed action, and Irish nationalists were marking the 50th anniversary of the 1916 Easter Rising. Some unionists warned that "a revival of the IRA was imminent."

May–June

The UVF carried out three attacks on Catholics in Belfast. In the first, a Protestant civilian (Matilda Gould) died when UVF members tried to firebomb the Catholic-owned pub beside her house but accidentally struck her home. In the second, a Catholic civilian (John Patrick Scullion) was shot dead as he walked home. In the third, the UVF opened fire on three Catholic civilians as they left a pub, killing one (Peter Ward, a native of the Republic of Ireland) and wounding the other two.

1968

20 June

Civil rights activists (including Stormont MP Austin Currie) protested against discrimination in the allocation of housing. A house in Caledon, County

Tyrone was illegally occupied by an unmarried Protestant woman (the secretary of a local Ulster Unionist Party (UUP) politician) who had been given the house ahead of Catholic families with children. The protesters were forcibly removed by the Royal Ulster Constabulary (RUC.)

24 August

Northern Ireland's first civil rights march was held. Many more marches would be held over the following year. Loyalists attacked some of the marches and organized counter-demonstrations in efforts to get the marches banned.

5 October

A Northern Ireland Civil Rights Association march was to take place in Derry. When the loyalist Apprentice Boys announced its intention to hold a march at the same place and time, the Government banned the civil rights march. When civil rights activists defied the ban, RUC officers surrounded the marchers and beat them indiscriminately and without provocation. Over 100 people were injured, including a number of MPs. This sparked two days of serious rioting in Derry between Catholics and the RUC.

9 October

About 2,000 students from Queen's University Belfast tried to march to Belfast City Hall in protest against police brutality on 5 October in Derry. The march was blocked by loyalists led by Ian Paisley. After the protest, a student civil rights group, The People's Democracy was formed.

1969

4 January

A People's Democracy march between Belfast and Derry was repeatedly attacked by loyalists. At Burntollet it was ambushed by 200 loyalists and off-duty police (RUC) officers armed with iron bars, bricks and bottles. The marchers claimed that police did little to protect them. When the march arrived in Derry it was broken up by the RUC, which sparked serious rioting between Irish nationalists and the RUC. That night, RUC officers went on a rampage in the Bogside area of Derry, attacking Catholic homes, threatening residents, and hurling sectarian abuse. Residents then sealed off the Bogside with barricades to keep the police out, creating "Free Derry".

March–April

Members of the UVF and UPV bombed water and electricity installations in Northern Ireland, blaming them on the dormant IRA and on elements of the civil rights movement. The loyalists intended to bring down the Ulster Unionist Party (UUP) Prime Minister of Northern Ireland, Terence O'Neill, who had promised some concessions to the civil rights movement. There were six bombings and all were widely blamed on the IRA. As a response, British soldiers were sent to guard installations. Unionist support for O'Neill waned, and on 28 April he resigned as Prime Minister.

17 April

People's Democracy activist Bernadette Devlin was the youngest woman ever elected to Westminster.

19 April

During clashes with civil rights marchers in Derry, RUC officers entered the house of an uninvolved Catholic civilian, Samuel Devenny, and beat him, along with two of his daughters. One of the daughters was beaten unconscious as she lay recovering from surgery. Devenny suffered a heart attack and died on 17 July from his injuries.

13 July

During clashes with nationalists throwing stones at an Orange Hall in Dungiven, RUC officers beat Francis McCloskey, a Catholic civilian (aged 67). He died of his injuries the next day.

5 August

The UVF planted their first bomb in the Republic of Ireland, damaging the RTE Television Centre in Dublin.

12–14 August

Battle of the Bogside

During an Apprentice Boys march, serious rioting erupted in Derry between Irish nationalists and the RUC. RUC officers, backed by loyalists, entered the nationalist Bogside in armored cars and tried to suppress the riot by using CS gas, water cannon and eventually firearms. The almost continuous rioting lasted for two days.

14–17 August

Northern Ireland riots of August 1969

In response to events in Derry, Irish nationalists held protests throughout Northern Ireland. Some of these became extremely violent. In Belfast, loyalists responded by attacking nationalist districts. Rioting also erupted in Newry, Armagh, Crossmaglen, Dungannon, Coalisland and Dungiven. Six Catholics and two Protestants were shot dead and at least 133 were treated for gunshot wounds. Scores of houses and businesses were burnt out, most of them owned by Catholics. Thousands of families, mostly Catholics, were forced to flee their homes and refugee camps were set up in the Republic. The British Army was deployed on the streets of Northern Ireland, which marked the beginning of Operation Banner.

11 October

Three people were shot dead during street violence in the loyalist Shankill area of Belfast. Two were Protestant civilians (George Dickie and Herbert Hawe) shot by the British Army and one was an RUC officer (Victor Arbuckle) shot by the UVF. Arbuckle was the first RUC officer to be killed in the Troubles. The loyalists had taken to the streets in protest at the Hunt Report, which recommended the disbandment of the B Specials and disarming of the RUC.

October–December

The UVF detonated bombs in the Republic of Ireland. In Dublin it detonated a car bomb near the Garda Síochána central detective bureau. It also bombed a power station at Ballyshannon, a Wolfe Tone memorial in

Bodenstown, and the Daniel O'Connell monument in Dublin. A split formed in the Irish Republican Army, creating two distinct groups, the Official IRA and the Provisional IRA.

1970

31 March

Following an Orange Order march, intense riots erupted on the Springfield Road in Belfast. Violence lasted for three days, and the British Army used CS gas for the first time in large quantities. About 38 soldiers and dozens of civilians were injured.

3 April

Ian Freeland the British Army's overall commander in Northern Ireland, announced that anyone throwing petrol bombs would be shot dead if they did not heed a warning from soldiers.

19 June

Edward Heath became Prime Minister of the United Kingdom after winning a majority in the general election.

27-28 June

Following the arrest of Bernadette Devlin, intense riots erupted in parts of Derry and Belfast. Further violence erupted in Belfast following Orange marches past Catholic neighborhoods. This led to gun battles between republicans and loyalists. Seven people were killed.

3–5 July

Falls Road Curfew.

A British Army raid in the Falls district of Belfast developed into a riot between soldiers and residents and then gun battles between soldiers and the 'Official' IRA. The British Army sealed off the area, imposed a 36-hour curfew and raided hundreds of homes under the cover of CS gas. Three

Catholic civilians (Charles O'Neill, William Burns and Patrick Elliman) as well as a British journalist of Polish descent, Zbigniew Uglik, were killed by the British Army, sixty others were injured, and 300 were arrested. Fifteen soldiers were shot by the OIRA.

2 August

Rubber bullets were used for the first time.

The constitutional nationalist Social Democratic and Labor Party (SDLP) was formed.

1971

3–6 February

Under pressure from the unionist government of Northern Ireland, the British Army began a series of raids in nationalist areas of Belfast, sparking three days of violence. On 6 February, British soldiers shot dead Catholic civilian Bernard Watt in Ardoyne and IRA member James Saunders in Oldpark, claiming both were armed. Shortly after, the IRA shot dead British soldier Robert Curtis during rioting in New Lodge. He was the first on-duty British soldier killed in the Troubles. The next day, James Chichester-Clark, Prime Minister of Northern Ireland, declared that "Northern Ireland is at war with the Irish Republican Army Provisionals."

9 March

Three off-duty Scottish soldiers (John McCaig, Joseph McCaig and Dougald McCaughey) were shot dead by the IRA after being lured from a pub in Belfast. Two days later, 4,000 loyalist shipyard workers took to the streets to demand the mass internment of Irish republicans.

23 March

Brian Faulkner became the Prime Minister of Northern Ireland.

25 May

The IRA threw a time bomb into Springfield Road British Army/RUC base in Belfast, killing British Army Sergeant Michael Willetts and wounding seven RUC officers, two British soldiers and eighteen civilians.

8 July

During street disturbances, British soldiers shot dead two Catholic civilians (Desmond Beattie and Seamus Cusack) in Free Derry. As a result, riots erupted in the city and the SDLP withdrew from Stormont in protest.

9–10 August

Operation Demetrius.

Internment without trial was introduced. Armed soldiers launched dawn raids throughout Northern Ireland, arresting 342 people suspected of being involved with the IRA. Most of those arrested were Catholics who had no links with republican paramilitaries, and many reported that they and their families were beaten and threatened by soldiers. This sparked four days of violence in which 20 civilians, two IRA members (Patrick McAdorey and Seamus Simpson) and two British soldiers were killed

Fourteen of the civilians, including a Catholic priest, Father Hugh Mullan, were killed by British soldiers; 11 of them in the Ballymurphy massacre. Winston Donnell (22) became the first Ulster Defence Regiment (UDR) soldier to die in 'the Troubles' when he was shot by the IRA near Clady, County Tyrone. An estimated 7,000 people, mostly Catholics, were forced to flee their homes. The introduction of internment caused a major, long-term increase in violence.

September

Loyalists formed the Ulster Defence Association (UDA). The group would quickly become the largest loyalist group in Northern Ireland.

4 December

McGurk's Bar bombing.

The UVF exploded a bomb at a Catholic-owned pub in Belfast, killing fifteen Catholic civilians (including two children) and wounding seventeen others. This was the highest death toll from a single incident in Belfast during the Troubles.

11 December

Balmoral Showroom bombing.

A bomb exploded outside a furniture showroom on the mainly Protestant and loyalist Shankill Road, Belfast. Four civilians, two adults (Hugh Bruce, a Protestant, and Harold King, a Catholic), and two babies, Tracey Munn (2 years old) and Colin Nichol (17 months old) were killed. The babies both died instantly when part of the wall crashed down upon the pram they were sharing. The adult employees were killed and nineteen people were wounded. The IRA was blamed.

1972

30 January

Bloody Sunday.

26 unarmed civilians were shot (of whom 13 were killed and one fatally wounded) by the British Army during a massive anti-internment demonstration in Derry. One of the dead, Gerard Donaghy, was a member of Fianna Éireann and reportedly had nail bombs on his person.

2 February

Funerals were held for eleven of those killed on Bloody Sunday. Prayer services were held across Ireland. In Dublin, over 30,000 marched to the British Embassy, carrying thirteen replica coffins and black flags. They attacked the Embassy with stones and bottles, then petrol bombs. The building was eventually burned to the ground.

22 February

Aldershot bombing.

Seven people were killed by an Official IRA car bomb at Aldershot Barracks in England. It was thought to be in retaliation for Bloody Sunday. Six of those killed were ancillary workers (five female and one male), and the seventh was a Roman Catholic British Army chaplain (Father Gerry Weston, aka Captain Gerard Weston, MBE), who had recently returned from service in Northern Ireland. The six others were Thelma Bosley, Margaret Grant, John Haslar, Joan Lunn, Jill Mansfield, and Cherie Munton.

4 March

Abercorn Restaurant bombing.

A bomb exploded in a crowded restaurant in Belfast, killing two Catholic civilians (Anne Owens and Janet Bereen) and wounding 130. Many were badly maimed. The IRA was blamed.

20 March

Donegal Street bombing.

The PIRA detonated its first car bomb, on Donegal Street in Belfast. Allegedly due to inadequate warnings, four civilians (Sydney Bell, Ernest Dougan, James Macklin, and Henry Miller), two RUC officers (Ernest McAllister and Bernard O'Neill) and a UDR soldier (Samuel Trainor) were killed while 148 people were wounded.

30 March

Northern Ireland's Government and Parliament were dissolved by the British Government. Direct rule from Westminster was introduced.

14 April

The PIRA exploded twenty-four bombs in towns and cities across Northern Ireland. There were fourteen shootouts between the PIRA and security forces.

22 April

An 11-year-old boy (Francis Rowntree) was killed by a rubber bullet fired by the British Army in Belfast. He was the first person to die from a rubber bullet impact.

13–14 May

Battle at Springmartin.

Following a loyalist car bombing of a Catholic-owned pub in the Ballymurphy area of Belfast, clashes erupted between the PIRA, UVF and British Army. Seven people were killed: five civilians (four Catholics, one Protestant), a British soldier, and a member of the Fianna Éireann (PIRA youth wing).

28 May

Four PIRA volunteers and four civilians were killed when a bomb they were preparing exploded prematurely at a house on Anderson Street, Belfast.

29 May

The Official IRA announced a ceasefire. This marked the end of the Official IRA's military campaign.

9 July

Springhill Massacre.

British snipers shot dead five Catholics (2 civilians, 2 members of Fianna Éireann, and a Roman Catholic priest) and wounded two others in Springhill, Belfast.

13 July

There was a series of gun-battles and shootings across Belfast. The PIRA shot dead three British Army soldiers (David Meeke, Kenneth Mogg, and Martin Rooney), and the British Army shot dead two civilians (Thomas Burns and Terence Toolan) and a PIRA volunteer (James Reid.)

14 July

There was a series of gun-battles and shootings across Belfast. The PIRA shot dead three British Army soldiers (Peter Heppenstall, John Williams and Robert Williams-Wynn). The British Army shot dead a PIRA volunteer (Louis Scullion) and an OIRA volunteer (Edward Brady), while a Protestant civilian (Jane McIntyre) was shot dead in crossfire.

21 July

Bloody Friday.

Within the space of 75 minutes, the PIRA exploded twenty-two bombs in Belfast, killing nine people: five civilians (William Crothers, Jackie Gibson, Thomas Killops, Brigid Murray, Margaret O'Hare and Stephen Parker), two British Army soldiers (Stephen Cooper and Philip Price) and one UDA volunteer (William Irvine) were killed, while 130 were injured.

31 July

Operation Motorman.

The British Army used 12,000 soldiers supported by tanks and bulldozers to re-take the "no-go areas" controlled by the PIRA.

31 July

Claudy bombing.

Nine civilians (five Catholics and four Protestants) were killed when three car bombs exploded in Claudy, County Londonderry. No group has since claimed responsibility but the late Father James Chesney, a local Catholic priest, who was the IRA's quartermaster and Director of Operations of the South Derry Brigade, was later implicated.

20 December

Five civilians, four Catholics (Bernard Kelly, Charles McCafferty, Francis McCarron, and Michael McGinley) and one Protestant (Charles Moore), were killed in gun attack on the Top of the Hill Bar, Strabane Old Road, Waterside, Derry. It is believed the UDA was responsible.

JOHN A. BRENNAN

1973

4 February

British Army snipers shot dead a PIRA volunteer and three civilians at the junction of Edlingham Street and New Lodge Road, Belfast.

7 February

The United Loyalist Council held a one-day strike to "re-establish some sort of Protestant or loyalist control over the affairs of the province". Loyalist paramilitaries forcibly tried to stop many people going to work and to close any businesses that had opened. There were eight bombings and thirty-five arsons. Three loyalist paramilitaries and one civilian were killed.

8 March

Old Bailey Bombing.

The PIRA undertook its first operation in England, when it planted four car bombs in London. Ten members of the PIRA team, including Gerry Kelly and the Price sisters, were arrested at Heathrow Airport while trying to leave the country.

17 May

Five British Army soldiers (Barry Cox, Frederick Drake, Arthur Place, Derek Reed, and Sheridan Young) were killed by a PIRA booby-trap bomb outside Knock-na-Moe Castle Hotel, Omagh, County Tyrone.

12 June

Coleraine bombings.

Six Protestant pensioners (Dinah Campbell, Francis Campbell, Elizabeth Craigmile, Nan Davis, Elizabeth Palmer and Robert Scott) were killed and 33 other people wounded by a PIRA car bomb on Railway Road, Coleraine, County Londonderry. The warning given before the explosion had been inadequate.

154

28 June

Northern Ireland Assembly elections took place.

31 October

Mountjoy Prison escape.

Three PIRA volunteers escaped from Mountjoy Prison in Dublin using a hijacked helicopter.

9 December

The Sunningdale Agreement was signed.

1974

4 February

M62 coach bombing.

Eight British Army soldiers and three civilians (the wife and two children of one of the soldiers who was killed) are killed when a PIRA bomb exploded on a bus as it was travelling along the M62 motorway in West Yorkshire, England.

4 March

Harold Wilson defeats Edward Heath in the general election to become British Prime Minister, it is his second time in office, the first being from 1964-1970.

20 April

The Troubles claimed its 1000th victim, James Murphy, a petrol station owner in County Fermanagh.

2 May

Six Catholic civilians (Francis Brennan, James Doherty, Thomas Ferguson, John Gallagher, William Kelly and Thomas Morrissey) were killed and eighteen wounded when the UVF exploded a bomb at Rose & Crown Bar on Ormeau Road, Belfast.

15 May

Beginning of the Ulster Workers' Council strike.

17 May

Dublin and Monaghan bombings.

The UVF exploded four bombs (three in Dublin, one in Monaghan) in the Republic of Ireland. They killed thirty-three civilians and wounded a further 300. This was the highest number of casualties in a single incident during "The Troubles". It has been alleged that members of the British security forces were involved. The UVF did not claim responsibility until 15 July 1993.

28 May

The Northern Ireland Executive collapsed. As a result, direct rule was re-introduced.

17 June

The Provisional IRA bombed the Houses of Parliament in London, injuring 11 people and causing extensive damage.

5 October

Guildford Pub bombings.

Four British soldiers (William Forsyth, Ann Hamilton, John Hunter and Caroline Slater) and one civilian (Paul Craig) were killed by PIRA bombs at two pubs in Guildford, England.

21 November

Birmingham pub bombings.

Twenty-one civilians were killed when bombs exploded at two pubs in Birmingham, England. This was the deadliest attack in England during the Troubles. The "Birmingham Six" would be tried for this and convicted. Many years later, after new evidence of police fabrication and suppression of evidence, their convictions would be quashed and they would be released.

10 December

The Irish National Liberation Army (INLA) and its political wing the Irish Republican Socialist Party (IRSP) was founded at the Spa Hotel in the village of Lucan near Dublin.

22 December

The PIRA announced a Christmas ceasefire. Before the ceasefire, they carried out a bomb attack on the home of former Prime Minister Edward Heath. Heath was not in the building at the time and no one was injured.

1975

10 February

The PIRA agreed to a truce and ceasefire with the British government and the Northern Ireland Office. Seven "incident centres" were established in nationalist areas to monitor the ceasefire and the response of the security forces.

20 February

A feud began between the Official IRA (OIRA) and the Irish National Liberation Army (INLA). The two groups assassinated a number of each other's volunteers until the feud ended in June 1975.

15 March

A feud began between the Ulster Volunteer Force (UVF) and Ulster Defence Association (UDA), resulting in a number of assassinations.

6 April

Daniel Loughran (18), then a member of the People's Liberation Army (PLA), which later became the Irish National Liberation Army (INLA), was shot dead at Divis Flats, Belfast, by members of the Official Irish Republican Army (OIRA) in the continuing feud between the OIRA and the INLA.

12 April

Six Catholic civilians were killed in a UVF gun and grenade attack on the Strand Bar in Belfast.

Paul Crawford (25), then a member of the Official Irish Republican Army (OIRA), was shot dead on the Falls Road, Belfast. This killing was another in the feud between the OIRA and the Irish National Liberation Army (INLA.)

22 June

The UVF tried to derail a train by planting a bomb on the railway line near

Straffan, County Kildare, Republic of Ireland. A civilian, Christopher Phelan, tried to stop the UVF volunteers, and was stabbed-to-death. His actions, however, reportedly delayed the explosion long enough to allow the train to pass safely.

17 July

Four British soldiers (Calvert Brown, Edward Garside, Robert McCarter, and Peter Willis) were killed by a PIRA remote-controlled bomb near Forkill, County Armagh. The attack was the first major breach of the February truce.

31 July

Miami Showband massacre.

UVF volunteers (some of whom were also UDR soldiers) shot dead three musicians (Tony Geraghty and Fran O'Toole, both from the Republic of

Ireland, and Brian McCoy, a Northern Irish Protestant), members of the Irish showband called the 'Miami,' at Buskhill, County Down. The gunmen staged a bogus military checkpoint, stopped the showband's minibus and ordered the musicians out. Two UDR soldiers (Harris Boyle and Wesley Somerville) hid a time bomb in the bus, but it exploded prematurely and they were killed. The other gunmen then opened fire on the musicians and fled. Three UDR soldiers were later convicted for their part in the attack, which has been linked to the 'Glenanne gang.'

13 August

Bayardo Bar attack.

PIRA volunteers carried out a gun and bomb attack on the Bayardo Bar, a pub in Belfast frequented by UVF commanders. Four Protestant civilians (Linda Boyle, William Gracey, Samuel Gunning, and Joanne McDowell), and one UVF member (Hugh Harris) were killed.

1 September

Five Protestant civilians (William Herron, John Johnston, Nevin McConnell, James McKee, and Ronald McKee) were killed and seven were wounded in a gun attack on Tullyvallen Orange Hall near Newtownhamilton, County Armagh. One of the Orangemen was an off-duty RUC officer, who returned fire. The attack was claimed by the South Armagh Republican Action Force (SARAF), which claimed it was retaliation for "the assassinations of fellow Catholics in Belfast."

2 October

The UVF killed seven civilians in a series of attacks across Northern Ireland. Six were Catholics (Frances Donnelly, Gerard Grogan, Marie McGrattan, Thomas Murphy, Thomas Osbourne, and John Stewart) and one was a Protestant (Irene Nicholson). Four UVF volunteers (Mark Dodd, Robert Freeman, Aubrey Reid, Samuel Swanson) were killed when the bomb they were transporting prematurely exploded as they drove along a road in Farrenlester, County Londonderry, near Coleraine.

22 November

Drummuckavall Ambush.

Three British Army soldiers (James Duncan, Peter McDonald and Michael Sampson) were killed and one soldier was wounded when the PIRA attacked a watchtower in Drummuckavall, Crossmaglen, South Armagh.

25 November

A loyalist gang nicknamed the "Shankill Butchers" undertook its first "cut-throat killing" (that of Francis Crossen). The gang was named for its late-night kidnapping, torture and murder (by throat slashing) of random Catholic civilians in Belfast.

5 December

End of internment.

6 December

Balcombe Street Siege.

For six days, four PIRA volunteers held two hostages at an apartment in London.

19 December

The Red Hand Commandos exploded a no-warning car bomb in Dundalk, killing two civilians (Jack Rooney and Hugh Watters) and wounding twenty. Shortly after, the same group launched a gun and bomb attack across the border in Silverbridge.

Two local Catholic civilians (Michael and Patrick Donnelly) and an English civilian (Trevor Brecknell), married to a local woman, were killed in that attack, while six others were wounded. The attacks have been linked to the notorious "Glenanne gang."

1976

4–5 January

Reavey and O'Dowd killings.

The UVF shot dead six Catholic civilians from two families (one group was a trio of brothers; the other was an uncle and two nephews) in coordinated attacks in County Armagh. An officer in the RUC Special Patrol Group took part in the killings, which have been linked to the "Glenanne gang."

5 January

Kingsmill massacre.

In retaliation for the Reavey and O'Dowd killings, the South Armagh Republican Action Force shot eleven Protestant men after stopping their minibus at Kingsmill, County Armagh. Ten died; one survived despite being shot 18 times.

23 January

The PIRA truce of February 1975 was officially brought to an end.

1 March

End of Special Category Status for prisoners convicted of terrorist crimes.

16 March

Harold Wilson announced his resignation as British Prime Minister, taking effect on 5 April 1976.

17 March

Four Catholic civilians, including two children (Patrick Barnard, Joseph Kelly, James McCaughey, and Andrew Small) were killed and twelve wounded when the UVF exploded a car bomb at Hillcrest Bar, Dungannon. The attack has been linked to the "Glenanne gang."

5 April

James Callaghan was elected leader of the Labour Party and succeeded Harold Wilson as Prime Minister of the United Kingdom.

15 May

The UVF launched gun and bomb attacks on two pubs in Charlemont, County Armagh, killing four Catholic civilians (Felix Clancy, Robert McCullough, Frederick McLoughlin, and Sean O'Hagan). A British Army UDR soldier was later convicted for taking part in the attacks. The PIRA killed three RUC officers in County Fermanagh and one RUC officer in County Down.

5 June

Nine civilians were killed during separate attacks in and around Belfast. After a suspected republican bombing killed two Protestant civilians (Robert Groves and Edward McMurray) in a pub, the UVF killed three Catholic civilians and two Protestant civilians, all males (Samuel Corr, James Coyle, Edward Farrell, John Martin, and Daniel McNeil) in the gun and bomb attack at the Chlorane Bar. In a separate bomb attack on the International Bar, Portaferry, County Down, the UVF killed a Catholic civilian. The UDA/UFF also assassinated a member of Sinn Féin, Colm Mulgrew.

15 June

Ruby Kidd (28), Francis Walker (17) and Joseph McBride (56), all Protestant civilians, were shot dead during a Republican Action Force gun attack on The Store Bar, Lyle Hill Road, Templepatrick.

2 July

Ramble Inn attack.

The UVF killed six civilians (five Protestants, one Catholic) in a gun attack at a pub near Antrim. The pub was targeted because it was owned by Catholics. The victims were Frank Scott, Ernest Moore, James McCallion, Joseph Ellis, James Francey (all Protestants) and Oliver Woulahan, a Catholic.

21 July

Christopher Ewart Biggs (the British Ambassador to Ireland) and his secretary Judith Cook were assassinated by a bomb planted in Mr. Biggs' car in Dublin. Two others in the car were seriously injured.

30 July

Four Protestant civilians were shot dead at a pub off Milltown Road, Belfast. The attack was claimed by the Republican Action Force.

10 August

A PIRA volunteer (Danny Lennon) was shot dead by the British Army as he drove along a road in Belfast. His car then went out of control and killed three children. This incident sparked a series of "peace rallies" throughout the month. The group that organised the rallies became known as Peace People, and was led by Mairead Corrigan and Betty Williams. Their rallies were the first (since the conflict began) where large numbers of Protestants and Catholics joined forces to campaign for peace.

14 September

Blanket protests began in the Maze prison, in protest at the end of special category status. The term 'blanket protest' comes from the protesters refusal to wear prison uniforms, instead wrapping blankets around themselves.

1977

11 December

Mairead Corrigan and Betty Williams received the Nobel Peace Prize.

1978

17 February

La Mon restaurant bombing.

Eleven civilians and an RUC officer were killed and thirty wounded by a PIRA incendiary bomb at the La Mon Restaurant near Belfast.

17 June

The PIRA killed an RUC officer (Hugh McConnell) and kidnapped and murdered another (William Turbitt), near Crossmaglen, County Armagh. The following day, loyalist paramilitaries kidnapped a Catholic priest and vowed to hold him hostage until the RUC officer was freed. However, they released the priest shortly thereafter under pressure from the authorities and church leaders. In December 1978 the kidnappers were charged with the kidnapping and the murder of a Catholic shopkeeper, William Strathearn.

21 June

The British Army shot dead three PIRA volunteers (Denis Brown, William Mailey, and James Mulvenna) and a passing UVF volunteer (William Hanna, in a case of mistaken identity) at a postal depot on Ballysillan Road, Belfast. It is claimed that the PIRA volunteers were about to launch a bomb attack.

21 September

The PIRA exploded bombs at the RAF airfield near Eglinton, County Londonderry. The terminal building, two aircraft hangars and four planes were destroyed.

14–19 November

The PIRA exploded over fifty bombs in towns across Northern Ireland, injuring thirty-seven people. Belfast, Derry, Armagh, Castlederg, Cookstown and Enniskillen were hardest hit.

1979

20 February

The Shankill Butchers.

Eleven loyalists known as the "Shankill Butchers" were sentenced to life in prison for nineteen murders. The gang was named for its late-night kidnapping, torture and murder (by throat slashing) of random Catholic civilians in Belfast.

22 March

The PIRA assassinated Richard Sykes, the British ambassador to the Netherlands, along with his valet, Karel Straub, in Den Haag. The group also exploded twenty-four bombs in various locations across Northern Ireland.

30 March

The INLA assassinated Airey Neave, Conservative MP and advisor to Margaret Thatcher. The INLA exploded a booby-trap bomb underneath his car as he left the House of Commons, London.

17 April

Four RUC officers were killed by a PIRA van bomb in Bessbrook, County Armagh. The bomb was estimated at 1000 lbs., believed to be the largest PIRA bomb used up to that point.

4 May

Margaret Thatcher of the Conservative Party wins a landslide victory to become Prime Minister of the United Kingdom defeating the Labour Party who were in power for six years.

27 August

Warrenpoint ambush.

Eighteen British Army soldiers were killed when the PIRA exploded two roadside bombs as a British convoy passed Narrow Water Castle near Warrenpoint. There was a brief exchange of fire, and the British Army shot dead a civilian. This was the British Army's highest death toll from a single attack during the Troubles. On the same day, four people (including Lord Mountbatten, a cousin of the Queen) were killed by a PIRA bomb on board a boat near the coast of County Sligo.

29 September

During a visit to the Republic of Ireland, Pope John Paul II appealed for an end to the violence in Northern Ireland.

16 December

Four British Army soldiers (Allan Ayrton, William Beck, Simon Evans, and Keith Richards) were killed by a PIRA landmine near Dungannon, County Tyrone. Another British Army soldier (Peter Grundy) was killed by a PIRA landmine near Forkill, County Armagh, and an ex-UDR soldier (James Fowler) was shot dead in Omagh.

1980

17 January

Dunmurry train explosion.

A PIRA bomb prematurely detonated on a passenger train near Belfast, killing two civilians (Mark Cochrane and Max Olorunda) as well as one of the bombers (Kevin Delaney), and severely injuring five (including the other bomber, Patrick Flynn).

10 June

Eight PIRA prisoners escaped from Crumlin Road Gaol in Belfast. Using handguns that had been smuggled into the prison, they took prison officers hostage and shot their way out of the building.

27 October

Republican prisoners in the Maze began a hunger strike in protest against the end of special category status.

18 December

First Republican hunger strike called off.

1981

21 January

Sir Norman Stronge and his son James Stronge (both former UUP MPs) were assassinated by the IRA at their home Tynan Abbey, which was then burnt down.

1 March

Republican prisoners in the Maze began a second hunger strike.

9 April

Hunger striker Bobby Sands won a by-election to be elected as a Member of Parliament at Westminster. The law was later changed to prevent prisoners standing in elections.

5 May

After 66 days on hunger strike, Sands died in the Maze. Nine further hunger strikers died in the following 3 months.

19 May

Five British Army soldiers (Michael Bagshaw, Paul Bulman, Andrew Gavin, John King, and Grenville Winstone) were killed when their Saracen APC was ripped apart by a PIRA roadside bomb at Chancellor's Road, Altnaveigh, near Bessbrook, County Armagh.

17 July

Glassdrummond Ambush.

The PIRA attacked a British Army post in South Armagh, killing one soldier (Lance Corporal Gavin Dean) and injuring another (Rifleman John Moore).

1 September

Northern Ireland's first religiously integrated secondary school opened.

3 October

Republican hunger strike ended.

1982

20 April

The PIRA exploded bombs in Belfast, Derry, Armagh, Ballymena, Bessbrook and Magherafelt. Two civilians were killed and twelve were injured.

20 July

Hyde Park and Regent's Park bombings.

Eleven British soldiers and seven military horses died in PIRA bomb attacks during military ceremonies in Regent's Park and Hyde Park, London. Many spectators were badly injured.

6 December

Droppin' Well bombing.

Eleven British soldiers and six civilians were killed by an INLA time bomb at the Droppin' Well Bar in Ballykelly, County Londonderry.

1983

11 April

In the first 'supergrass' trial, fourteen UVF volunteers were jailed for a total of two hundred years.

May

New Ireland Forum set up.

13 July

Four British Army (Ulster Defence Regiment) soldiers (Ronald Alexander, Thomas Harron, John Roxborough, and Oswald Neely), all Protestant members of the 6th Battalion Ulster Defence Regiment, were killed when their vehicle struck a PIRA landmine near Ballygawley, County Tyrone.

5 August

In another 'supergrass' trial, twenty-two PIRA volunteers were jailed for a total of over four thousand years. Eighteen would later have their convictions quashed.

25 September

Maze Prison escape.

Thirty-eight republican prisoners staged an elaborate escape from the Maze Prison in County Antrim. One prison officer died of a heart attack after being stabbed by an escapee, and twenty others were injured, including two shot with guns that had been smuggled into the prison. Half of the escapees were recaptured within two days. Another drowned in County Fermanagh while trying to evade the police after the escape. Others were later captured but some evaded capture in the Republic of Ireland or the United States.

17 December

Harrods bombing.

A PIRA car bomb outside a department store in London killed six people, three civilians (Philip Geddes, Jasmine Cochrane-Patrick, and Kenneth Salvesen, a United States citizen), and three police officers, Sergeant Noel Lane, Constable Jane Arbuthnot and Inspector Stephen Dodd. Another policeman lost both legs and 90 people were injured. The PIRA's Army Council claimed that it had not authorized the attack.

1984

21 February

Two PIRA volunteers (Henry Hogan and Declan Martin) and a British soldier (Paul Oram) were killed during a shootout in Dunloy, near Ballymoney, County Antrim.

18 May

Three British soldiers (Thomas Agar, Robert Huggins, and Peter Gallimore) were killed by a PIRA landmine in Enniskillen, County Fermanagh. Two RUC officers were killed by a PIRA landmine near Camlough, South Armagh.

12 October

Brighton Hotel bombing.

The PIRA carried out a bomb attack on the Grand Hotel, Brighton, which was being used as a base for the Conservative Party Conference. Five people, including Sir Anthony Berry, a Member of Parliament, died in the bombing, and others were maimed or injured. Prime Minister Margaret Thatcher escaped harm.

14 December

Ian Thain became the first British soldier to be convicted of murdering a civilian during the Troubles.

1985

28 February

Newry mortar attack.

A PIRA mortar attack on an RUC base in Newry killed nine officers and wounded thirty-seven. This was the RUC's highest death toll from a single attack during the Troubles.

20 May

Four RUC officers (David Baird, Tracy Doak, Stephen Rodgers, William Wilson) were killed on mobile patrol by a PIRA remote-controlled bomb near Killeen, County Armagh.

15 November

Margaret Thatcher and Garret FitzGerald signed the Anglo-Irish Agreement.

All fifteen Unionist MPs at Westminster resigned in protest against the Anglo-Irish agreement.

7 December

Attack on Ballygawley barracks.

The PIRA launched an assault on the RUC barracks in Ballygawley, County Tyrone. Two RUC officers (Constable George Gilliland and Reserve Constable William Clements) were killed. The barracks was completely destroyed by the subsequent bomb explosion and three other RUC officers were injured.

1986

23 June

Northern Ireland Assembly was officially dissolved

August

The PIRA issued a warning that anyone working with the security forces in Northern Ireland would be considered "part of the war machine" and would be "treated as collaborators."

2 November

During the Sinn Féin Ard Fheis (party conference) in Dublin, a majority of delegates voted to end the party's policy of abstentionism – refusing to take seats in Dáil Éireann (Irish parliament). This led to a split and Ruairí Ó Brádaigh, Dáithí Ó Conaill and approximately 100 people staged a walk-out. The two men would form a new party called Republican Sinn Féin.

10 November

Loyalists held a closed meeting at the Ulster Hall in Belfast. The main speakers at the meeting were Ian Paisley, Peter Robinson and Ivan Foster. During the meeting a new organisation, Ulster Resistance, was formed to "take direct action as and when required" to end the Anglo-Irish Agreement.

1987

8 May

Loughgall Ambush.

Eight PIRA volunteers and one civilian were killed by the Special Air Service (SAS) in Loughgall, County Armagh. The eight-strong PIRA unit had just exploded a bomb at the RUC base when it was ambushed by the 24-strong SAS unit.

8 November

Remembrance Day bombing.

Eleven civilians and an RUC officer were killed and sixty-three others were wounded by a PIRA bomb during a Remembrance Day service in Enniskillen, County Fermanagh. One of those killed was Marie Wilson. In an emotional BBC interview, her father Gordon Wilson (who was injured in the attack) expressed forgiveness towards his daughter's killer, and asked Loyalists not to seek revenge. He became a leading peace campaigner and was later elected to the Irish Senate.

1988

11 January

SDLP leader John Hume and Sinn Féin leader Gerry Adams held a meeting.

6 March

Operation Flavius.

Three PIRA volunteers (Daniel McCann, Seán Savage and Mairéad Farrell) were killed by the SAS in Gibraltar.

16 March

Milltown Cemetery attack.

At the funeral of those killed in Gibraltar, Loyalist Michael Stone (using pistols and grenades) attacked the mourners, killing one PIRA volunteer (Caoimhín Mac Brádaigh, a.k.a. Kevin Brady), and two civilians (Thomas McErlean and John Murray). More than 60 others were wounded. Much of the attack was filmed by television news crews.

19 March

Corporals killings.

At the funeral of Caoimhín Mac Brádaigh (aka Kevin Brady), who was killed in the Milltown Cemetery attack, two non-uniformed British Army corporals (David Howes and Derek Wood) were mistaken for loyalist gunmen and attacked by civilians after driving a car into the funeral procession. The two were later shot dead by the IRA.

15 June

Lisburn van bombing.

Six off-duty British Army soldiers (Signalman Mark Clavey, Lance Corporal Derek Green, Lance Corporal Graham Lambie, Corporal Ian Metcalf, Corporal William Patterson, and Sergeant Michael Winkler) were killed by a PIRA bomb attached to their van in Lisburn. The bomb was designed to ensure it exploded upwards, lowering the risk of collateral damage.

20 August

Ballygawley bus bombing.

Eight British Army soldiers (Blair Bishop, Peter Bullock, Jayson Burfitt, Richard Greener, Alexander Lewis, Mark Norsworthy, Stephen Wilkinson, and Jason Winter) were killed and twenty-eight wounded when the PIRA attacked their bus with a roadside bomb near Ballygawley, County Tyrone.

19 October

The British Government introduced the broadcasting ban on organizations believed to support terrorism, including 11 Loyalist and Republican groups and Gerry Adams' voice.

1989

12 February

Republican solicitor Pat Finucane was assassinated by the Ulster Freedom Fighters. He was shot dead in front of his wife and two sons.

22 September

Deal barracks bombing.

Eleven British military bandsmen were killed by a PIRA bomb at Deal Barracks in Kent, England.

8 October

Twenty-eight members of the British Army (Ulster Defence Regiment) were arrested on suspicion of leaking security force documents to loyalist paramilitaries.

13 December

Attack on Derryard checkpoint.

Using machine guns, grenades and a flamethrower, the PIRA launched an assault on a British Army checkpoint near Rosslea, County Fermanagh, killing two British soldiers (Private James Houston and Lance-Corporal Michael Paterson). Two other soldiers were injured, one more severely than the other.

1990

9 April

Four British Army (Ulster Defence Regiment) soldiers were killed when the PIRA exploded a landmine under their patrol vehicle in Downpatrick, County Down. The blast was so powerful that the vehicle was hurled into a nearby field.

6 May

Operation Conservation.

The British Army attempted to ambush a PIRA unit in South Armagh, but were counter-ambushed; one British soldier was killed.

20 July

The PIRA bombed the London Stock Exchange.

24 July

A PIRA landmine attack on an RUC patrol vehicle in Armagh killed three RUC officers (William Hanson, David Sterritt, and Joshua Willis) and a civilian (Sister Catherine Dunne, a Roman Catholic nun from Dublin).

30 July

Conservative MP for Eastbourne, Ian Gow, was assassinated by a PIRA bomb planted in his car.

30 September

Two Catholic civilians (Martin Peake and Karen Reilly) were killed by British Army soldiers in Belfast.

24 October

Proxy bomb attacks.

The PIRA launched three "proxy bombs" or "human bombs" at British Army checkpoints. Three men (who were or had been working with the British Army) were tied into cars loaded with explosives and ordered to drive to each checkpoint. Each bomb was detonated by remote control. The first exploded at a checkpoint in Coshquin, killing the driver and five soldiers. The second exploded at a checkpoint in Killeen, County Armagh; the driver, James McAvoy, narrowly escaped, albeit suffered a broken leg but one soldier (Fusilier Andrew Grundy) was killed and 23 other soldiers were wounded. The third failed to detonate.

22 November

Margaret Thatcher resigned as British Prime Minister.

1991

3 February

The PIRA launched a "proxy bomb" attack on a British Army (Ulster Defense Regiment) base in Magherafelt, County Londonderry. The bomb caused major damage to the base and nearby houses, but the driver escaped before it exploded.

7 February

The PIRA launched three mortar shells at 10 Downing Street while the British Cabinet were holding a meeting. The shells landed in a garden. No members of the cabinet were injured, although four people received minor injuries, including two police officers.

3 March

Cappagh killings.

Three PIRA volunteers (Malcolm Nugent, Dwayne O'Donnell, John Quinn) and a Catholic civilian (Thomas Armstrong) were shot dead by the UVF at Boyle's Bar in Cappagh, County Tyrone. A 21-year-old man was badly wounded. The volunteers arrived in a car as a UVF gang was about to attack the pub. The UVF fired at the car (killing the volunteers) then fired into the pub (killing the civilian) but the alleged target, Brian Arthurs (brother of late PIRA volunteer Declan Arthurs, who was killed at Loughgall) escaped.

29 April

The Combined Loyalist Military Command (CLMC) (acting on behalf of all loyalist paramilitaries) announced a ceasefire lasting until 4 July. This was to coincide with political talks between the four main parties (the Brooke-Mayhew talks.)

31 May

Glenanne barracks bombing.

The PIRA launched a large truck bomb attack on a British Army (Ulster Defence Regiment) base in County Armagh. Three soldiers (Lance Corporal Robert Crozier and Privates Paul Blakely and Sydney Hamilton) were killed; ten soldiers and four civilians were wounded. The blast left a deep crater and it could be heard over 30 miles away. Most of the UDR base was destroyed by the blast and the fire that followed. It was one of the largest bombs detonated during the Troubles in Northern Ireland.

3 June

Coagh ambush.

The SAS shot dead three PIRA volunteers (Tony Doris, Lawrence McNally and Michael "Pete" Ryan) as they traveled in a car through Coagh, County Tyrone. The car burst into flames.

1992

17 January

Teebane bombing.

A PIRA landmine killed eight Protestant men and wounded six others at Teebane Crossroads near Cookstown, County Tyrone. The men had been working for the British Army at a base in Omagh and were returning home on a minibus. The PIRA said that the men were legitimate targets because they had been "collaborating" with the "forces of occupation". Shortly thereafter, Peter Brooke (Secretary of State for Northern Ireland) appeared on the Irish RTÉ Late-Late Show and was persuaded to sing "Oh My Darling, Clementine". Unionists accused him of gross insensitivity for agreeing to do so.

4 February

Allen Moore, a RUC officer from Comber, reportedly distraught by the killing of a colleague, Constable Norman Spratt, walked into a Belfast Sinn Féin office and shot dead two Sinn Féin activists, Patrick Loughran (61) and Patrick McBride (aged 40), and one civilian, Michael O'Dwyer (aged 24), all Catholics. Moore drove away from the scene and later shot himself.

5 February

Sean Graham bookmakers' shooting.

The UDA, using the covername "Ulster Freedom Fighters" (UFF), claimed responsibility for a gun attack on a bookmaker's shop on Lower Ormeau Road, Belfast. Five Catholic men and boys were killed (Christy Doherty, Jack Duffin, James Kennedy, Peter Magee, and William McManus). Nine others were wounded, one critically. This was claimed as retaliation for the Teebane bombing on 17 January 1992. In November 1992, the UDA carried out another attack on a betting shop in Belfast, killing three Catholic civilians and wounding thirteen.

16 February

Clonoe ambush.

A PIRA unit attacked Coalisland RUC base in County Tyrone using a heavy machine gun mounted on the back of a stolen lorry. Following the attack, the British Army ambushed the unit in a graveyard. Four PIRA volunteers (Peter Clancy, Kevin Barry O'Donnell, Seán O'Farrell, and Patrick Vincent) were killed and two were wounded but escaped.

10 April

The PIRA exploded a truck bomb at the Baltic Exchange in London. Despite a telephoned warning, three civilians were killed. The bomb caused £800 million worth of damage.

1 May

Attack on Cloghoge checkpoint.

The PIRA, using a van modified to run on railway tracks, launched an elaborate bomb attack on a British Army checkpoint in South Armagh. The checkpoint was obliterated. One soldier (Fusilier Andrew Grundy) was killed and 23 others were wounded

17 May

Coalisland riots.

After a PIRA bomb attack on a British Army patrol near Cappagh, County Tyrone, in which a soldier lost his legs, British soldiers raided two public houses in Coalisland and caused considerable damage. This led to a fist-fight between the soldiers and locals. Shortly thereafter, another group of British soldiers arrived and fired on a crowd of civilians, wounding seven.

28 August

The PIRA's "South Armagh snipers" undertook their first successful operation, when a British Army soldier (Private Paul Turner) was shot dead on patrol in Crossmaglen, County Armagh.

23 September.

The PIRA exploded a 2000 lb. bomb at the Northern Ireland Forensic Science Laboratory in South Belfast. The laboratory was obliterated, seven hundred houses were damaged, and 20 people were injured. The explosion could be heard from over 16 km away. It was one of the largest bombs to be detonated during the Troubles in Northern Ireland.

1993

26 February

Warrington bomb attacks.

A bomb exploded at a gas storage facility in Warrington. It caused extensive damage but no injuries. While fleeing the scene, the bombers shot and injured a police officer and two of them were then caught after a high-speed car chase.

20 March

Second Warrington bomb attack.

After a telephoned warning, the PIRA exploded two bombs in Warrington, Cheshire, England. Two children (Johnathan Ball and Tim Parry) were killed and fifty-six people were wounded. There were widespread protests in Britain and Ireland following the deaths.

25 March

Castlerock killings.

The UDA, using the covername "Ulster Freedom Fighters" (UFF), claimed responsibility for shooting dead four Catholic civilians and a PIRA volunteer at a building site in Castlerock, County Londonderry. Later in the day it claimed responsibility for shooting dead another Catholic civilian in Belfast.

24 April

Bishopsgate bombing.

After a telephoned warning, the PIRA exploded a large bomb at Bishopsgate, London. It killed one civilian, wounded thirty others, and caused an estimated £350 million in damage.

23 October

Shankill Road bombing.

Eight civilians, one UDA volunteer and one PIRA volunteer were killed when a PIRA bomb prematurely exploded at a fish shop on Shankill Road, Belfast. The PIRA's intended target was a meeting of loyalist paramilitary leaders, which was scheduled to take place in a room above the shop. However, unbeknownst to the PIRA, the meeting had been re-scheduled.

30 October

Greysteel massacre.

The UDA, using the covername "Ulster Freedom Fighters" (UFF), claimed responsibility for a gun attack on the Rising Sun Bar in Greysteel, County Londonderry. Eight civilians (six Catholic, two Protestant) were killed and twelve wounded. One gunman yelled "trick or treat!" before he fired into the crowded room; a reference to the Halloween party taking place. The UFF claimed that it had attacked the "nationalist electorate" in revenge for the Shankill Road bombing.

1994

11 January

The broadcasting ban on Sinn Féin was lifted in the Republic of Ireland.

10 March

The PIRA carried out a mortar attack on Heathrow Airport, London. Further attacks were carried out later in the month, but on each occasion, the mortars failed to explode.

2 June

Twenty-nine people, including ten senior RUC officers, died during the 1994 Scotland RAF Chinook crash at Mull of Kintyre, Scotland. They were travelling from Belfast to a security conference in Inverness.

16 June

Shankill Road killings.

The INLA shot dead three UVF volunteers (Colin Craig, David Hamilton, and Trevor King) in a gun attack on Shankill Road, Belfast.

18 June

Loughinisland massacre.

The UVF shot dead six Catholic civilians (Eamon Byrne, Barney Greene, Malcolm Jenkinson, Daniel McCreanor, Patrick O'Hare, and Adrian Rogan) and wounded five others during a gun attack on a pub in Loughinisland, County Down.

31 August

The Provisional Irish Republican Army (PIRA) issued a statement which announced a complete cessation of military activities. This ceasefire was broken less than two years later.

16 September

The broadcasting ban was lifted in the UK.

13 October

The Combined Loyalist Military Command (CLMC) issued a statement which announced a ceasefire on behalf of all loyalist paramilitaries. The statement noted that "The permanence of our cease-fire will be completely dependent upon the continued cessation of all nationalist/republican violence."

1995

16 January

A delegation from Sinn Féin met with officials from the Northern Ireland Office.

22 February

The British and Irish governments released the Joint Framework document.

17 March

Gerry Adams attended a reception held by Bill Clinton at the White House.

3 July

Lee Clegg, a British Army paratrooper, was released from prison on the orders of Secretary of State Patrick Mayhew. Clegg had been jailed in 1993, for the murder of Catholic teenager Karen Reilly.

8 September

David Trimble was elected as the leader of the Ulster Unionist Party, following the resignation of James Molyneaux.

1996

9 February

London Docklands bombing.

After a telephoned warning, the PIRA bombed the Docklands in London. The bomb killed two civilians (Inam Bashir and John Jeffries) and injured 39 others. It brought an end to the ceasefire after 17 months and 9 days.

10 June

Political talks at Stormont began without Sinn Féin.

15 June

Manchester bombing.

After a telephoned warning, the PIRA exploded a bomb in Manchester, England. It destroyed a large part of the city center and injured over 200 people. To date, it is the largest bomb to be detonated on the British mainland since the Second World War. There were no fatalities.

7 July

Drumcree conflict.

The RUC decided to block the annual Orange Order march through the nationalist Garvaghy area of Portadown. In response, loyalist protestors attacked the RUC and blocked hundreds of roads across Northern Ireland. Eventually, the RUC allowed the march to continue, leading to serious rioting by nationalists across Northern Ireland.

7 October

The Provisional IRA exploded two bombs at the British Army HQ in Thiepval Barracks, Lisburn. A British soldier, Warrant Officer James Bradwell, died four days later of his wounds. 31 other people were wounded.

1997

12 February

A PIRA sniper shot dead a British soldier (Lance Bombardier Stephen Restorick) manning a checkpoint in Bessbrook, County Armagh. He was the last British soldier to be killed during Operation Banner.

5 April

The Grand National horse race was cancelled, and Aintree Racecourse evacuated following a hoax bomb warning from the PIRA. The race was eventually run several days later, 7 April, without disruption.

1 May

Tony Blair becomes UK Prime Minister after winning the biggest landslide victory in UK political history ending 18 years of Conservative rule.

6 June

Sinn Féin won its first ever seats in Dáil Éireann (Irish Parliament)

16 June

The PIRA shot dead two RUC officers (John Graham and David Johnston) on patrol, Church Walk, Lurgan, County Armagh. They were the last RUC officers killed before the signing of the Belfast Agreement.

6–9 July

Drumcree conflict.

To ensure the Orange Order march could continue, the security forces sealed-off the nationalist Garvaghy area of Portadown. This sparked serious rioting in Portadown and across nationalist areas in Northern Ireland. After four days, the RUC released figures which showed that there had been 60 RUC officers injured; 56 civilians injured; 117 people arrested; 2,500 plastic bullets fired; 815 attacks on the security forces; 1,506 petrol bombs thrown; and 402 hijackings. This was the last time that the Orange Order's parade through nationalist areas around Drumcree was permitted by the authorities.

20 July

The PIRA renewed its ceasefire.

9 September

Sinn Féin signed the Mitchell Principles.

Multi-party talks resumed.

27 December

INLA prisoners shot dead Loyalist Volunteer Force (LVF) leader and fellow prisoner Billy Wright inside the maximum-security Maze Prison. The LVF launched a number of revenge attacks over the following weeks.

1998

10 April

After two years of intensive talks, the Belfast Agreement (also known as the 'Stormont Agreement' or 'Good Friday Agreement') was signed at Stormont in Belfast.

15 May

The Loyalist Volunteer Force (LVF) declared an "unequivocal ceasefire". The group hoped this would encourage people to vote against the Belfast Agreement.

22 May

Two referendums were held on the Belfast Agreement, one in Northern Ireland and one in the Republic of Ireland. In Northern Ireland the vote was 71.2% in favor, in the Republic of Ireland the vote was 94.39% in favor.

25 June

Northern Ireland Assembly elections were held. David Trimble was elected First Minister. Seamus Mallon was elected deputy.

5–12 July

Drumcree conflict.

The annual Orange Order march was prevented from marching through the nationalist Garvaghy area of Portadown. Security forces and about 10,000 loyalists began a standoff at Drumcree church. During this time, loyalists launched 550 attacks on the security forces and numerous attacks on Catholic civilians. On 12 July, three children were burnt to death in a loyalist petrol bomb attack. This incident brought an end to the standoff.

15 August

Omagh bombing.

A dissident republican group calling itself the Real IRA exploded a bomb in Omagh, County Tyrone. It killed twenty-nine civilians (one of whom was pregnant with twins), making it the worst single bombing of the Troubles, in terms of civilian life lost.

22 August

The Irish National Liberation Army (INLA) declared a ceasefire.

16 October

John Hume and David Trimble jointly awarded the Nobel Peace Prize.

The year 1998 is considered by many as the end of the troubles. Violence nonetheless continues on a small-scale basis.

1999

27 January

Former IRA volunteer and "supergrass" Eamon Collins was found dead near Newry, County Down. The South Armagh IRA were believed to have been responsible.

15 March

Solicitor Rosemary Nelson, who had represented the Garvaghy residents in the Drumcree dispute, was assassinated by a booby trapped car bomb in Lurgan, County Armagh. A loyalist group, Red Hand Defenders, claimed responsibility.

8 August

The INLA and its political wing the IRSP stated that "There is no political or moral argument to justify a resumption of the campaign."

1 December

Direct rule officially ended as power was handed over to the Northern Ireland Assembly.

2000

11 February

Direct rule was reinstated and the Northern Ireland Assembly suspended by new Secretary of State for Northern Ireland Peter Mandelson, citing insufficient progress on decommissioning.

27 March

The Bloody Sunday Inquiry began in Derry. It is the biggest public inquiry in British history.

29 May

Devolution was restored to the Northern Ireland Assembly.

2–12 July

Drumcree conflict.

The annual Orange Order parade was banned from marching through the nationalist Garvaghy area of Portadown. The security forces erected large barricades to prevent loyalists from entering the area. About 2,000 British soldiers were deployed to keep order. During the standoff at Drumcree Church, loyalists continually launched missiles at the security forces.

28 July

The final prisoners were released from the Maze Prison, under the conditions of the Good Friday Agreement.

21 September

The Real IRA (RIRA) fired a rocket propelled grenade at MI6 headquarters in London, causing superficial damage.

2001

4 March

BBC bombing.

A Real IRA bomb exploded outside BBC Television Centre, causing some damage to the building.

19 June

Holy Cross dispute.

RUC officers had to protect pupils and parents at Holy Cross Catholic Girls' School in Belfast, following attacks from loyalist protesters. The attacks resumed in September, following the school summer holidays, before subsiding in January 2002.

11–13 July

The worst rioting for several years took place in Belfast.

3 August

Ealing bombing.

A Real IRA car bomb injured seven civilians in Ealing, west London.

23 October

The Provisional IRA began decommissioning of its weaponry.

4 November

The RUC was replaced by the Police Service of Northern Ireland (PSNI). Recruits were recruited on the basis of 50% Catholic, 50% Protestant.

2005

12 July

Police were attacked with blast and petrol bombs during rioting in the Ardoyne area of Belfast, following an Orange Order parade. Eighty police officers were injured and several people were arrested.

28 July

The PIRA issued a statement declaring it has ended its armed campaign and will verifiably put its weapons beyond use.

26 September

International weapons inspectors issue a statement confirming the full decommissioning of the PIRA's weaponry.

11–12 September

Following the rerouting of a controversial Orange Order Parade, rioting broke out in Belfast on a scale not seen for many years.

30 October

The Loyalist Volunteer Force (LVF) instructed its forces to "stand down".

2006

February

Serious rioting broke out all across Dublin City.

24 November

Michael Stone was arrested for breaking into the Stormont parliament buildings while armed. He would receive 16 years' imprisonment for attempting to murder Martin McGuinness and Gerry Adams.

2007

7 March

Elections to the Northern Ireland Assembly took place.

26 March

DUP leader, Ian Paisley and Sinn Féin leader, Gerry Adams meet face-to-face for the first time, and the two come to an agreement regarding the return of the power-sharing executive in Northern Ireland.

3 May

The UVF and RHC issued a statement declaring an end to its armed campaign. The statement noted that they would retain their weapons but put them "beyond reach."

8 May

The new Northern Ireland Assembly met and the new Northern Ireland Executive was formed.

31 July

The British military's campaign in Northern Ireland (codenamed Operation Banner) officially ends.

11 November

The UDA issued a statement declaring an end to its armed campaign. It noted that they would retain their weapons but put them "beyond use."

2008

16 August

The Continuity IRA (CIRA) fired a rocket-propelled grenade at a police patrol in Lisnaskea, County Fermanagh. Three officers required hospital treatment.

25 August

Riots erupted in Craigavon, during which a number of vehicles were hijacked and shots were fired. The Independent Monitoring Commission blamed the CIRA for orchestrating the violence.

2009

7 March

Two British Army soldiers (Patrick Azimkar and Mark Quinsey) were shot dead and two others were seriously injured during a gun attack at Massereene Barracks in County Antrim. The dissident Real IRA (RIRA) claimed responsibility. These were the first British military fatalities in Northern Ireland since 1997.

9 March

A Catholic police officer (formerly RUC, then PSNI), Stephen Carroll, was shot dead in Craigavon, County Armagh. The CIRA claimed responsibility. This was the first police fatality in Northern Ireland since 1998. Police were petrol bombed when arrests were made. In the following week there were sporadic attacks on police by youths.

27 June

It was announced that the Ulster Volunteer Force (UVF) and the Red Hand Commando (RHC) had decommissioned their weapons.

11 October

The INLA formally vow to pursue its aims through peaceful political means, saying their "armed struggle is over."

2010

6 January

It was announced that the Ulster Defence Association (UDA) had decommissioned its weapons in front of independent witnesses.

6 February

It was announced that the Irish National Liberation Army (INLA) had decommissioned its weapons in front of independent witnesses.

9 February

The Independent International Commission on Decommissioning stood down.

22 February

The RIRA were blamed for detonating a car bomb outside a courthouse in Newry, heavily damaging the guard hut. This was the first successful car bomb attack in Northern Ireland since 2000.

12 April

A group calling itself Óglaigh na hÉireann claimed responsibility for detonating a car bomb outside the MI5 headquarters at Palace Barracks in Holywood, County Down.

23 April

A car bomb exploded outside a PSNI station in Newtownhamilton, County Armagh.

28 May

The UVF were blamed for shooting dead former Red Hand Commando member Bobby Moffett in broad daylight on Shankill Road, Belfast. The killing put the UVF's claims of weapons decommissioning and commitment to peace under serious scrutiny.

3 August

Óglaigh na hÉireann claimed responsibility for detonating a 200 lb. car bomb outside Strand Road PSNI station in Derry.

4 October

The RIRA claimed responsibility for detonating a car bomb near the Ulster Bank on Culmore Road, Derry.

6 November

Three PSNI officers were injured after a grenade was thrown at them on Shaw's Road, Belfast. Óglaigh na hÉireann claimed responsibility.

2011

2 April

Ronan Kerr, a 25-year-old Catholic PSNI officer, was killed after a bomb exploded under his car in Omagh, County Tyrone. The Real IRA claimed responsibility.

17–20 May

Queen Elizabeth II's visit to the Republic of Ireland.

May–July

Irish republicans in Maghaberry Prison took part in a dirty protest.

June–July

Northern Ireland riots.

27 June

Queen Elizabeth II shook hands with Sinn Féin MLA and former IRA commander Martin McGuinness.

12 July

North Belfast riots.

There was rioting in the Ardoyne area of Belfast following the Orange Order's Twelfth marches. Up to 20 PSNI officers were injured and a number of shots were fired by republicans.

26 July

The Real IRA announced that it was merging with Republican Action Against Drugs and other independent dissident republican groups.

2–4 September

Loyalists attack a republican parade organized by Republican Network for Unity in north Belfast, sparking three nights of rioting between nationalists and loyalists in the area of Carlisle Circus. More than 60 PSNI officers were injured.

1 November

A Prison Officer was shot dead on the M1 motorway near Craigavon while driving to work. The shots were fired from another car, which drove alongside. The Real IRA claimed responsibility and said it was a response to the treatment of republican prisoners holding a dirty protest at Maghaberry Prison. He was the first Prison Officer to be killed since 1993.

4 December

Belfast City Hall flag protests.

Belfast City Council votes to only fly the Union Jack from Belfast City Hall on designated days. Since 1906, it had been flown every day of the year. This sparked protests by loyalists throughout Northern Ireland, some of which became violent. The protests and rioting continued into 2013.

2013

12–17 July

Rioting by loyalists occurred across Belfast and across of Northern Ireland after an Orange Order parade was prevented by the PSNI from passing the nationalist Ardoyne shop fronts in North Belfast during The Twelfth celebrations, in accordance with a Parades Commission ruling. During which loyalists attacked with petrol bombs, blast bombs and even reportedly ceremonial swords. There were clashes between loyalist and nationalist crowds. 71 PSNI officers including 3 mutual aid officers from Britain were injured in the days of rioting, and during disorder on 12 July DUP MP Nigel Dodds was injured after he was knocked unconscious by a brick thrown by loyalists. 62 people involved in the rioting were arrested across Northern Ireland.

2016

4 March

A prison officer (Adrian Ismay) died from a heart attack in a hospital on 4 March 2016. He had been seriously wounded by a booby-trap bomb which detonated under his van on Hillsborough Drive, East Belfast 11 days earlier. These wounds were directly responsible for the heart attack that killed him. The 'New' IRA claimed responsibility and said it was a response to the alleged mistreatment of republican prisoners at Maghaberry Prison. It added that the officer was targeted because he trained prison officers at Maghaberry.

Read more here:

https://en.wikipedia.org/w/index.php?title=Timeline_of_the_Northern_Ireland_Troubles_and_peace_process&oldid=741738025

Appendix

Chapter 3

The New Kingdoms.

1   The Uí Tuirtri, meaning "descendants of Tort" were based east of the
     Sperrin Mountains in eastern County Derry and Tyrone.

2   The Uí Maic Cairthinn, meaning "descendants of Cairthend" settled
     south of Lough Foyle in north-western County Derry.

3   The Uí Fiachrach Arda Sratha, meaning "descendants of Fiachrach of
     Ard Straw" were based at Ardstraw in modern-day County Tyrone.

4   The Uí Cremthainn, based in what is now parts of modern-day County
     Fermanagh, Monaghan, and Tyrone.

5   The Uí Méith, based in modern-day County Monaghan.

6   The Airthir, meaning "Priestly" were based around the city of Armagh,
     and held control of the offices of the church in Armagh, which had pre-
     eminence in Ireland.

7   The Mugdorna, based originally in County Monaghan, re-located to
     southern County Down, and named the area after themselves. Their
     name lives on as "Mourne", the present-day name for the area and the
     Mourne Mountains.

8   The Fir Chraíbe, also known as the Fir na Chraíbe, meaning "men of the
     branch" were located west of the River Bann in north-eastern County
     Derry.

9   The Fir Lí, also known as the Fir Lee, meaning "people of Lí" were
     located west of the River Bann in mid-eastern County Derry.

10   Another dynasty, the Uí Moccu Úais were composed of members of
     three tribes namely, the Uí Tuirtri, the Uí Maic Cairthinn and the Uí
     Fiachrach Arda Sratha, and were collectively known as the Uí Moccu
     Úais, eventually moved their bases to Counties Meath and Westmeath
     and near to the old kingdom of Brega.

Chapter 9

Penal Laws

As discussed in Chapter 9, a number of penal laws were passed during the sixteenth and seventeenth centuries. Below is an example of such laws.

- Exclusion of Catholics from most public offices, Presbyterians were also barred from 1707.
- Ban on intermarriage with Protestants.
- Presbyterian marriages were not legally recognized by the state.
- Catholics barred from holding firearms or serving in the armed forces.
- Barred from membership in the Parliaments of Ireland and England from 1652.
- Disenfranchising Act 1728, exclusion from voting until 1793;
- Catholics exclusion from the legal professions and the judiciary.
- Education Act 1695 – ban on foreign education.
- Ban on Catholics and Protestant Dissenters entering Trinity College Dublin.
- On a death of a Catholic, his legatee could benefit by conversion to the Church of Ireland.

The Popery Acts were essentially designed to control how land was to be granted, inherited and/or distributed. As you can see from the list below, many of these acts were used to discriminate against Catholics.

- Catholic inheritances of land were to be equally subdivided equally between an owner's sons.
- Ban on converting from Protestantism to Roman Catholicism.
- Ban on Catholics buying land under a lease of more than 31 years.
- Ban on custody of orphans being granted to Catholics on pain of 500 pounds fine.
- Ban on Catholics inheriting Protestant land.
- Prohibition on Catholics owning a horse valued at over £5.
- Roman Catholic lay priests must register to preach under the Registration Act 1704.
- Catholic churches to be built from wood, not stone, and away from main roads.

- No person of the popish religion shall publicly or in private houses teach school, or instruct youth in learning within this realm upon pain of twenty pounds fine and three months in prison.
- Any and all rewards not paid by the crown for alerting authorities of offences to be levied upon the Catholic populace within parish and county.

Bibliography

Chapter 1

*Information regarding the earlier inhabitants is contained in the Book of Invasions:*https://archive.org/details/leborgablare01macauoft

Macalister, Robert Alexander Stewart. *Lebor gabála Érenn: the book of the taking of Ireland*. Vol. 1. Dublin: Published for the Irish Texts Society by the Educational Co. of Ireland, 1938.

Lebor gabála Érenn: The Book Of The Taking Of Ireland compiles a narrative history of the different colonists of Ireland and synthesizes some eleven manuscripts consisting of various redactions. What began as a history of the peoples then dominant in the country became a history of Ireland as a whole, tracing the evolution of languages, cultures, and descriptions that changed as Latin was translated into Irish and the *Lebor gabála Érenn* came to be regarded as a true history of the land and the peoples who called Ireland home.

Further information may be obtained from the Annals of the four Master.

See also www.ucc.ie/celt/published/T100005As

O'Donovan, John. *Annals of the Four Masters*. CELT: Corpus of Electronic Texts.

Annals of the Four Masters was known originally as *Annála ríoghachta Éireann* ('Annals of the kingdom of Ireland'). It came to be named after the 'Four Masters' since John Colgan applied this term to Franciscan friar Mícheál Ó Cléirigh and his three chief assistants, although two other scribes were involved in the project. The collection was compiled, in two successive stages, between 1632 and 1636. Its entries range from the Deluge (2,242 years after Creation) to AD 1616. As one of the principal Irish-language sources for Irish history up to 1616, they list names, dates, and (later) detailed historical accounts for which the authors had first-hand references.

Chapter 2

"Irish-society." Irish-Society. Accessed September 06, 2017.
https://www.irish-society.org/
See also: http://www.irish-society.org/.../groups-organizations/

This non-political affiliation of individuals is committed to learning more
about Irish history and its heritage. It maintains the Hedgemaster Archives, a
collection of Irish cultural and historical references. The collection includes
Irish storytelling, historical accounts, places, artifacts, and other links to
documents such as the Book of Kells and the Ogham alphabet, discovered in
China some 5,000 years ago. This society maintains information on groups,
organizations and peoples of Ireland throughout all phases of its history.

Chapter 3

Mac Niocaill, Gearóid , trans. *The Annals of Tigernach*. Paris, 1895.

The Annals of Tigernach mixes Latin, Old, and Middle Irish languages and
covers prehistoric times from the 12th century onward; but its real
importance lies in its coverage of the periods from 489-766, 973–1003 and
1018–1178, in the 14th century. Fragments partially attributed to
Tigernach Ua Braín, chronicle battles, individual births and deaths, and kings
and rulers, and chronicle the evolution of writings about Irish history during
these early times.

Keating, Geoffrey, and David Comyn. *The History of Ireland*. London: Nutt,
1987.

The History of Ireland is a 3-volume set originally written in 17th century Gaelic
by Dr. Keating. The first volume begins with the earliest recorded history to
the coming of St. Patrick, covering legends, ancient peoples, oral history and
battles. Volume 2 picks up where the first volume concluded, continuing to
to the Norman invasions with further Irish history and folk culture details on
the Viking Age, the High Kings, and the time of   Saints and Scholars. Book
3 is the master index for all the volumes and includes genealogical and family

tree references along with its discussion of ancient genealogies and the locations of clans with ancient pedigrees and family trees.

See also the Annals of Tigernach
https://www.ucc.ie/celt/published/T100002A/index.html
Additional information gathered from Geoffrey Keating's History of Ireland:
https://www.ucc.ie/celt/keat_cunn.html

Chapter 4

MacAirt, Seán. *The annals of Inisfallen: (Ms. Rawlinson B 503).* Dublin: Dublin Institute for Advanced Studies, 1988.

This coverage of the medieval history of Ireland holds some 2,500 entries that cover the years between 433 and 1450, was written by some 39 monks of Innisfallen Abbey, and synthesizes information from different sources around Munster as well as including a short narrative of the history of pre-Christian Ireland up to Saint Patrick. They were compiled around 2015 and were written in a combination of Irish and Latin. Today they are located in the Bodleian library in Oxford.

Chapter 5

Maguire, Cathal MacMaghnusa, Rory OCassidy, W. M. Hennessy, and Batholomew MacCarthy. *Annala Uladh = Annals of Ulster: otherwise, Annala Senait, Annals of Senat: a chronicle of Irish affairs.* Dublin: Printed for H.M. Stationery Off., by A. Thom, 1887.

The entries in the Annals of Ulster cover the period from AD 431 to AD 1540, with early entries (up to AD 1489) written by 15th century scribe Ruaidhrí Ó Luinín and later   entries (up to AD 1540) added by other scholars. Entries up to the mid-sixth used earlier   annalistic and historical texts, while later entries had their roots in oral history accounts.   They were written in Irish and Latin, but because the Annals copied its sources verbatim, they hold particular interest to scholars of history and linguistics alike, forming the basis   for later annals and accounts. Rules, kingdoms and important places in Ireland are documented, including a large amount of historical information on the invasions of the Vikings into Ireland, battles surrounding their appearance, and foreigner appearances on Irish soil.

Mageoghegan, Conall, and Denis Murphy. *The Annals of Clonmacnoise; Being The Annals Of Ireland From The Earliest Period to A.D. 1408*. Dublin: Printed for the Royal   Society of Antiquaries of Ireland, 1896.

The Annals of Clonmacnoise, an early 17th-century Early Modern English translation of a   lost Irish chronicle, covered the history of Ireland and the areas surrounding Conmacnoise from prehistory to the year 1408 (although several periods of history are missing, from 1182 to 1199 and again from 1290 to 1299). It was translated into English in 1627.

See also the following references:

1.   *The Annals of Clonmacnoise*
      https://archive.org/details/annalsofclonmacn00royauoft
2.   *The Annals of Innisfallen*
      https://www.ucc.ie/celt/published/T100004
3.   *The Annals of Ulster*
      https://www.ucc.ie/celt/published/T100001A/index.html

Chapter 6

Macalister, Robert Alexander Stewart. *Lebor Gabála Érenn: The Book Of The Taking Of Ireland*. Dublin: The Educational Company of Ireland, 1939.

There is no singular author or production for *Lebor Gabála Érenn: The Book Of The Taking Of Ireland,* which collects poetic and prose narratives docu menting Irish history and Irish peoples from the start of time to the Middle Ages. Several versions combine   narratives written by various authors from stories that developed over centuries, with a   focus on Ireland's settlement/conquest six times by six groups of people: the Cessair, the Partholón, the Nemed, the Fir Bolg, the Tuatha Dé Danann, and the Milesians. Modern scholars regard the *Lebor Gabála* as primarily myth rather than history, as it incorporates Irish pagan mythology and is written in such a manner as to provide epic drama rather than a strictly historical focus.

See also the Book of Invasions

1. www.ucc.ie/celt/indexLG.html
2. www.ancienttexts.org/library/celtic/irish

Irish Texts Archive. Accessed September 06, 2017.
http://www.ancienttexts.org/library/celtic/irish

The Academy for Ancient Texts is an reference website whose goal is to provide the largest on-line library of ancient texts in the world. Its link to Celtic/Irish references contains specialized information and documents that range from stories and adventures from Celtic literature and folk history to a collection of Celtic texts provided by Mary Jones, which translates key historical documents. From kingship genealogy to battles, births, deaths and wooings of major Celtic figures, and stories of daily life in   early Ireland, this archive presents source materials invaluable to the early history of the country.

Chapter 7

Gascoigne, Bamber. "History of Ireland" HistoryWorld. From 2001, ongoing.
http://www.historyworld.net/wrldhis/PlainTextHistories.asp?ParagraphID=fuf

Historyworld's 'History of Ireland' is written by Bamber Gascoigne and gathers Irish history into a series of interactive narratives and timelines. The overview for this portion of Chapter 7 begins with the Norman incursions: 1169-1170 and ends with the strengthening of three major Anglo/Irish families in the 14th - 15th century.

See also www.historyworld.net/wrldhis/PlainTextHistories.asp?ParagraphID=fuf

Chapter 8

Information on the O'Neill clan from Cardinal Tomas O'Fiach's book

O'Fiaich, Tomás. *The O'Neills of the Fews*. [Armagh] : Cumann Seanchais Ard Mhacha, [2003]/

The O'Neill dynasty is a group of Irish Gaelic families that have held prominent positions in Ireland as High Kings, sovereign kings and landowners, and various realms that merged with the Kingdom of Ireland. Many were prominent figures in Irish history. Cardinal Tomas O'Fiach's received in MA in early and medieval Irish history. *The O'Neills of the Fews* compiles Cardinal O Fiaich's articles in Seanchas Ard Mhacha.

Creggan History Society - Home Page. Accessed September 06, 2017. http://www.fuls.org.uk/cregganhistory/

The Creggan Local History Society was formed in 1985 with the goal of collecting and distributing information on the history of the Creggan Parish in particular and of South Armagh in general. It provides an archive of historical material, publishes a historical journal, and has produced ten historical journals and a host of other publications.

See also

1. *'The O'Neils of the Fews'*
      www.worldcat.org/title/oneills-of-the-fews/oclc/58723745
2. *Creggan Historical Society*
      www.fuls.org.uk/cregganhistory

Chapters 9-11

Gascoigne, Bamber. "History of Ireland" HistoryWorld. From 2001, ongoing.http://www.historyworld.net/wrldhis/PlainTextHistories.asp?ParagraphID=fuf
Historyworld's 'History of Ireland' is written by Bamber Gascoigne and gathers Irish history into a series of interactive narratives and timelines.

See also

History of Ireland
1.   *www.historyworld.net/wrldhis/PlainTextHistories.asp?ParagraphID=juf*

2.   *From Wikipedia*
     https://en.wikipedia.org/wiki/History_of_Ireland_(1691—1801)

"History of Ireland (1691–1801)." Wikipedia. August 30, 2017. Accessed
September 06, 2017
https://en.wikipedia.org/wiki/History_of_Ireland_1691-1891. Wikipedia,
the free encyclopedia, offers an extensive review of the early history of
Ireland from 1691-1801, following the evolution of Anglo-Irish families
whose ancestors   settled in Ireland after its conquest by England, and
traces the elements influencing Irish politics, laws, culture, and religion.
References and a bibliography accompany a history that provides a
foundation for understanding Ireland's influences and evolution.

Chapters 12-13

"The History of 20th Century Ireland." Your Irish Culture. Accessed
September 06, 2017. http://www.yourirish.com/history/20th-century/

The website yourirish.com began as a hobby, created for some friends in the
U.S., and evolved into a global history and culture informational site. It
gathers stories, information, and Irish history and provides an informative
and entertaining read for Irish families around the world. The 'History of
20th Century Ireland' section focuses on Irish events ranging from the
founding of Northern Ireland's civil rights movement to the Republic of
Ireland Act in 1949, Irish participation in World War II from 1939-1945, to
the presence of British troops in Ireland.

The Roll of the Kings: Book of Leinster version. Accessed September 06,
2017. http://www.ancienttexts.org/library/celtic/ctexts/lebor6.html

The *Book of Leinster* is a medieval Irish manuscript written between 1151 and
1201, with the bulk of the work probably completed in the 1160s. The
portion of it which contains a roll of Irish kings provides a history of Irish

royalty in the oldest existent chronology of Irish kingship, from
the princedoms of Ireland, and of their times, from the era of the Sons of Míl
to the time of Túathal Techtmar. How the kings assumed power over
Ireland, battles fought between them, verses that follow princes, victories,
and their fates after victory, and a timeline of the princes and times of
Ireland provides a complete coverage of early Irish royalty.

Royal Society of Antiquaries of Ireland . Accessed September 06, 2017.
http://rsai.ie/

The Royal Society of Antiquaries of Ireland (RSAI) was established in 1849
with a mandate to 'preserve, examine all ancient monuments and memorials
of the arts, manners and customs of the past.' Their membership supports
research studies and includes an extensive library of early Irish documents of
Irish history and archaeology, including archival photographs, antiquarian
sketches, drawings, and manuscripts. It also publishes an international journal
and organizes lectures and events involving Irish antiquaries.

See History of Ireland www.yourirish.com/history/20th-century

ABOUT THE AUTHOR

Irish Author and Poet John Anthony Brennan is a native of Crossmaglen, a small, tough town in County Armagh, Ireland. A town, like Ireland herself, which has survived much pain and hardship through the centuries beneath the invaders harsh heel. His first book, "Don't Die with Regrets: Ireland and the Lessons my Father Taught me" was chosen as winner in the 'Next Generation Indie Book Awards' in 2015. It was also chosen as a finalist in the 'Worldwide Book Excellence Awards' in 2016. His second book titled, "The Journey: A Nomad Reflects" is his first poetry collection and continues his life story in a series of free verse and rhythmic narrative. "The Journey: A Nomad Reflects" has been chosen as a finalist in the 'Worldwide Book Excellence Awards' for 2016.

John's latest book titled, "Out of the Ice," is a history of Ireland which starts at the end of the last ice age and chronicles the many and varied cultures that inhabited an infant Ireland. It follows through and recounts many of the lesser known historic events that shaped Irish culture, century by century. The story brings the reader to the present day.

John's writings are a representation of a life's journey and are intended to inspire and inform the reader of a long-forgotten Ireland, its connection with the wider world, and the deep-rooted history embedded in the island's rocks and soil. The author has visited most of the sacred sites in this world and is convinced that a common thread connects them. He incorporates his experiences in his works and some of his writing expresses the spiritual dimension. He writes prose, short stories and poetry and performs his works at many venues in Ireland, New York and Long Island.

Blessings out of buffetings

Christians are never far from home and from the eternal joy and glory which will be their reward in heaven'. The reward will not be something they have earned because, in John Calvin's words, 'The promise of the reward is free'. All the Christian's rewards in heaven are his by the sovereign grace of a loving Father. What those rewards will be are beyond our imagining or understanding - as Thomas Watson says, 'The reward is as far above your thoughts as it is beyond your deserts.'

In the last book in the Bible, however, God turns back a corner of the curtain and in a series of metaphors gives us a glimpse of the glory that awaits those who have faithfully passed through the pressures of life: 'Therefore, they are before the throne of God and serve him day and night in his temple; and he who sits on the throne will spread his tent over them. Never again will they hunger; never again will they thirst. The sun will not beat upon them, nor any scorching heat. For the Lamb at the centre of the throne will be their shepherd; he will lead them to springs of living water. And God will wipe away every tear from their eyes' (Revelation 7:15-17).

Nothing that has ruined man's life on earth will be allowed to do so in heaven and opposition to God's people will be a thing of the past there. In A W Pink's phrase, 'One breath of paradise will extinguish all the adverse winds of earth.' This is the only context within which the persecution of God's people can be properly seen. In 1858 a young American clergyman by the name of Dudley Tyng died as the result of an accident on his parents' farm. In his last words to his father he asked him to tell all his fellow ministers to 'stand up for Jesus'. A few days after his death, one of his closest friends, fellow minister George Duffield, wrote a poem based on Tyng's last words. Duffield's poem eventually became a well-known Christian hymn, and the exhortation and encouragement of its closing lines provide the perfect climax to our study of the Beatitudes:

Stand up, stand up for Jesus!
The strife will not be long;
This day the noise of battle,
The next the victor's song.

To him that overcometh
A crown of life shall be;
He with the King of glory
Shall reign eternally.